Multiple
Personality
Disorder
from the
Inside Out

Multiple Personality Disorder from the Inside Out

edited by

Barry M. Cohen
Esther Giller
Lynn W.

Sidran

THE SIDRAN PRESS
211 Southway
Baltimore, MD 21218

Grateful acknowledgement is made for permission to
reprint an excerpt from *Children With Emerald Eyes* by
Mira Rothenberg. Copyright © 1987, Mira Rothenberg;
reprinted on page 76 by permission of the author.

International Standard Book Number: 0-9629164-0-4
Library of Congress Card Catalogue Number: 91-60530.
Printed in the United States of America.

Designer: Alan Carter
Cover concept: Robin B.
Cover photograph: © copyright 1991 Aaron M. Levin
Illustrations: p. 16, Robin B.; all other drawings, Janet H.

To those who shared their lives by contributing prose, poetry, and art.

And to all those who didn't,
but whose collective experience is illuminated in these pages.

Healing from MPD is like putting a puzzle together
without seeing the picture on the box.
—Amie R.

Who am we really and how do I talk about myselves?
—Gregory B.

I do not wish to commit death
But, oh how hard it is to commit life!
—Margaret O.

CONTENTS

ACKNOWLEDGMENTS

The editors of this book wish to thank the following people for their expertise, time, and invaluable support: Mary Allman and Linda Blick, of the Chesapeake Institute, for their faith in the project; Alan Carter, for design; Craig M. Gendler, for legal advice and comic relief; Wendy Harris and Robert L. Warren, of the Johns Hopkins University Press, for their encouragement and technical advice on publishing matters; Mary Medland for guidance and proofreading; Craig Hankin and Anne Mills for always listening; Dr. Richard Kluft, Dr. Frank Putnam, Dr. Colin Ross, the Troops, and Chris Sizemore, for direction, suggestions and comments; and to Dr. Joan Turkus, for introducing the editors, thereby making this book possible.

INTRODUCTION

About This Book

This book about "life with MPD" grew out of a crucial need for information by clients, supportive family members, and significant others. At this time, with the exception of several client-generated periodicals, there is very little material available about Multiple Personality Disorder written in a manner accessible to lay readers. While no single book can be all things to all people, this contribution to the literature is made in the hope of serving many purposes for many people.

Multiple Personality Disorder from the Inside Out is a product of the cooperation and common vision of the principals of three recently founded organizations devoted to improving the environment for individuals with MPD. The idea for this volume was born in late 1989 to Barry M. Cohen, M.A., A.T.R., art therapist and Program Director of the Abuse and Dissociative Disorders Recovery Unit at Dominion Hospital in Falls Church, Virginia. As founder and chairman of the Eastern Regional Conference on Abuse and Multiple Personality, Barry envisioned a booklet of writings by clients for conference attendees.

He approached Lynn W., 1991 affiliate member-at-large of the International Society for the Study of Multiple Personality and Dissociation (ISSMP&D) Executive Board, and editor and publisher of *MANY VOICES*, an MPD and Dissociative Disorders client-written newsletter, who agreed to distribute an initial questionnaire in an issue of that publication. Lynn volunteered to receive and coordinate the submitted material, and ultimately did the lioness's share of the organizational editing.

Simultaneously, Barry proposed the project to Esther Giller, director of The Sidran Foundation, a non-profit group active since 1988, which is concerned with abuse of the mentally ill and mental illnesses caused by abuse. The Sidran Foundation, approving the venture wholeheartedly, established the Sidran Press and undertook the publishing of this book.

In May 1990, a simple questionnaire was mailed to approximately 2,300 people: subscribers of *MANY VOICES* and members of the ISSMP&D, the professional organization of therapists treating MPD. The questionnaire addressed three relatively open-ended questions to clients, and one to their significant others. The questions were: "What do you wish you had known about MPD when you were first diagnosed?," "What would you like therapists to know about the experience of MPD?," and "What do you think spouses, friends, and/or supportive family members should know about MPD?" Significant others were asked, "What would you like to share with other friends and supportive family members of individuals with MPD?" Responses came from over 150 people, representing 32 states and Canada.

During the preliminary editing of the contributions, it became clear that the information elicited by these questions was much more broad-ranging than anticipated. The quantity of worthwhile information and the impact of the subject matter combined to influence a decision not to constrain the messages of the writers to fit a pre-conceived format, but rather to expand the book to tell the emerging story. All the writings contributed to this book were read and evaluated by Barry, Lynn, and Esther (a clinician, a survivor, and a family member), with the goal of selecting the material that would best serve the needs of each of the three audiences they represent. The contributions were eloquent and compelling. In the end, writings of 132 individuals were included in this book, 115 from women and 17 from men.

The bulk of the text of this book comes directly from those people most familiar with MPD: the ones who live with it. People with Dissociative Disorders tend to be intelligent, creative, resourceful, and articulate.

Their priceless perspective and personal insight enable the rest of us to view their worlds "from the inside out." Contributors are identified by first name and last initial unless they have specifically requested that full names or pseudonyms be used.

The experiences and opinions of these people may, occasionally, seem to contradict one another. The variety in their stories simply highlights the diversity and spectrum of dissociative multiplicity and the life experience that engenders. More significant, in fact, are the similarities found in their experiences: the fear of stigma, the resistance of the mental health world to accept the diagnosis, and prejudices against MPD (by survivors as well as the general public) caused by sensationalized media portrayals. (Almost half of these contributors wrote that their difficulties in accepting their MPD diagnoses were compounded by the contrast between their own lives and those depicted of "Eve" and "Sybil.") The opinions expressed in this book are those of the clients and their significant others, and not necessarily those of the editors or the therapeutic community.

The collection of writings has been organized by general themes. There is some overlap in the subject matter; many segments pertain to more than one chapter. Chapter 1 deals with the MPD diagnosis, and the range of reactions to it: from denial to fear and humiliation to relief. The working title for this chapter was "We're not crazy; we just lead complicated lives." The "not crazy" theme is a recurring one.

Chapter 2 addresses the physical and emotional pain of confronting the past as well as dealing with an MPD diagnosis. Writings about child abuse, ritual torture, and families of origin have been included in this chapter. Much of this material is highly emotional, and difficult to read; the struggle with despair finds its voice here. Vulnerable individuals may want to read this section with a supportive person.

Skepticism from outsiders further undermines acceptance of the diagnosis of MPD, and compounds isolation. Skepticism from within the medical or mental health communities can lead a reluctant consumer to inappropriate treatment. Chapter 3 discusses the mutual resentment that builds between people with MPD and skeptical mental health professionals, as well as the "vanishing friend syndrome."

Two chapters on therapy offer point/counterpoint views of the experience. After finding the "right" therapist, most individuals with MPD agree that treatment—though a long and difficult journey—is the true road to healing. Their varied comments about the therapeutic process are valuable learning tools for professionals and lay readers alike. The most frequently recurring themes are those of trust, control, and boundary-setting. Unfortunately, many individuals with Dissociative Disorders encounter the "wrong" clinicians, dubious treatment, or re-traumatization in the guise of therapy. Chapter 5 might be entitled "Straight Talk for Therapists"; in these pages, aching personal accounts illuminate the pitfalls of misdirected treatment.

The fact of survival among individuals with MPD celebrates their will to prevail and ultimate hope for healing. The high rate of recovery in treatment (as opposed to the deterioration common to Schizophrenia, for instance) is a relief to some. Others, experiencing the small triumphs of early-stage cooperation within their systems, feel buoyed by the prospect of the future. Growing confidence in their abilities to make decisions and to take responsibility for their healing contributes to the hope expressed in Chapter 6.

"Unification" is a chapter about a controversial topic. Some therapists consider integration the primary goal of MPD therapy; some clients don't even want to hear the word mentioned. Chapter 7 explores the range of emotions tied to unification issues: the grief of losing alters, the aspirations to wholeness, and the fear of the unknown, unified self.

The last two chapters are about people with Dissociative Disorders relating to friends and family, and vice versa. These contributions make it clear that support is perhaps as important to healing as therapy. Comments on whom to tell and how much information to share seem to vary with the degree of support and acceptance. Chapter 8 is filled with suggestions on how to ease the frictions of daily life. Chapter 9 is not written by people who have Dissociative Disorders, but rather by those who live with them. Most of the segments in this chapter are written by spouses, two are by adult children, and one is by a non-offending parent. Their concerns, frustrations, and supportive suggestions truly reflect the significance of others.

Readers who are diagnosed with MPD themselves may choose to think of these writings as a measuring stick against which they can compare and contrast their own experiences. Spouses and friends may benefit from the sense of community found in these pages; it may be reassuring for them to know that others in similar circumstances are prevailing. Professionals, novice and experienced in MPD and its course of treatment, may find here the wisdom of a collective voice, and structures upon which to build alliances.

How To Use This Book

This book is intended primarily for use by survivors, but also for spouses, friends, nurses, therapists, and anyone wishing to have a better understanding of MPD and the related Dissociative Disorders. Survivors might share it with therapists and spouses. Therapists might share it with clients and colleagues.

The chapters in the book can be used in many ways:

By clinicians—

—as a catalyst to help bring up difficult subjects for discussion.

—as a structure for discussion in a group therapy format.

By survivors—

—to validate personal experiences.

—to temper frustration brought on by a sense of isolation.

—to inspire journal keeping and creative writing.

—to clarify issues and feelings that may aid their healing process.

By spouses and significant others—

—to gain insight into the complex, painful, and often frightening world of loved ones.

—to educate themselves in order to more effectively help their MPD loved one get appropriate diagnosis and treatment.

About Multiple Personality Disorder and Dissociation

The great French psychiatrist Pierre Janet coined the word *disaggregation* about one hundred years ago to identify changes in consciousness which disturbed the normal, well-integrated functions of identity, memory, and thought in several of his patients. This term was later translated from the French as *dissociation*.

Janet's studies of patients with amnesias, fugues, and "successive existences" (now known as alter personalities), convinced him that their symptoms were the effect of split-off parts of the personality which were capable of independent thoughts, actions and identities. Further, he concluded that the dissociation which caused the symptoms was the result of past traumatic experiences, and that the symptoms could be alleviated by bringing the split-off memories and feelings into consciousness. Dr. Janet's contemporaries, both American and European, expanded upon his research and a model for the diagnosis and treatment of dissociation was soon built.[1] During the 1930s, however, as Freud's theories were embraced by the psychiatric world, studies of dissociation declined. Renewal of interest among the professional community was not sparked again until the 1980s, following increased public and professional awareness of child abuse and the rise in treatment of Vietnam veterans' post-traumatic stress syndromes.[2]

Most clinicians believe that dissociative processes exist on a continuum. At one end are mild dissociative experiences common to most people (such as daydreaming or highway hypnosis). At the other extreme is severe, chronic dissociation which may result in serious impairment or inability to function. There is a wide range of experiences in between. Some people with MPD can hold highly responsible jobs, contributing to society in a variety of professions, the arts, and public service. To co-workers, neighbors, and others with whom they interact daily, they apparently function normally.

Dissociation is normal in children, as anyone who has observed an imaginative, three-year-old can attest. When faced with highly anxiety-provoking situations from which there is no physical escape, the child may resort to "going away" in his or her head. This ability is typically used by children as an extremely effective defense against acute physical and emotional pain caused by highly traumatic situations, most commonly severe abuse. Over time, for a child who has been repeatedly abused, dissociation becomes reinforced and conditioned. The dissociative process may result in a series of discrete states which eventually may take on identities of their own. Often referred to as alternate personalities, these are the internal members of the MPD system. Changes between these personalities, or states of consciousness, are described as switching.

Dissociation and switching may become automatic responses to anxiety and anticipated anxiety, even in non-abusive situations. Even after the traumatic circumstance is long past, the vestigial pattern of defensive dissociation remains. Chronic defensive dissociation may lead to serious dysfunction in work, social and daily activities.

Individuals most likely to develop MPD present several factors in a common profile. They have endured repetitive, overwhelming, and often life-threatening trauma at a sensitive developmental stage of childhood (usually before the age of nine), and they may possess a biological predisposition for auto-hypnotic phenomena (a high level of hypnotizability). MPD is often referred to as a highly creative survival technique, because it allows individuals enduring "hopeless" circumstances to preserve some areas of healthy functioning.

Fortunately, the problems caused by dissociation are highly responsive to treatment, and people with MPD and other Dissociative Disorders can improve their lives through appropriate therapy.

Multiple Personality Disorder is one of four Dissociative Disorders identified in the *Diagnostic and Statistical Manual of Mental Disorders: Third Edition—Revised* (DSM-III-R), published by the American Psychiatric Association. It is significant to note that the 1980 edition of the *Manual* was the first to include MPD and the other Dissociative Disorders, indicating the very recent "legitimacy" of the diagnosis within the psychiatric community. However, many mental health professionals remain skeptical about the existence of Dissociative Disorders, compounding difficulties of survivors in getting appropriate diagnosis and treatment.

MPD survivors often spend years living with misdiagnoses, consequently floundering within the mental health system. They change from therapist to therapist and from medication to medication, getting treatment for symptoms but making little or no actual progress. This is not surprising, since the list of presenting symptoms of MPD reads like the *DSM-III-R* itself: depression, mood swings (alter shifts), suicidality, sleep disorders (usually night terrors and sleep walking), panic attacks and phobias (reactions to stimuli or "triggers"), alcohol and drug abuse, compulsions and rituals, psychotic-like symptoms (including auditory and visual hallucinations), and eating disorders. In addition, individuals with MPD experience headaches, amnesias, time loss, fugues, trancing, and out of body experiences. Some people with MPD have a tendency toward self-persecution, self-sabotage and even violence (both self-inflicted and outwardly directed).

There is a great deal of overlap of symptoms and experiences (such as time loss, amnesias, flashbacks, etc.) among the Dissociative Disorders. For the sake of clarity, this book will primarily focus on MPD, generally considered the most complex manifestation of dissociation. Readers are encouraged to apply relevant information regardless of their particular dissociative diagnosis.

Additional clinical information about MPD and definitions of specialized terminology are included in the Glossary at the back of this book. For those wishing to learn more, or in need of specific, detailed information, the list of books and articles in the Resource Guide may help.

[1] Putnam, Frank W., *Diagnosis and Treatment of Multiple Personality Disorder*, NY: Guilford Press, 1989, 1–4.
[2] Putnam, 5–6.

1

DIAGNOSIS

The sweetest words I ever heard were "No, you're not crazy . . . You're a walking miracle!"
—Vicki G.

MPD is not just a made-for-TV story. It is real. It makes you hurt and feel lonely. It makes you cry. I wish more people would understand.
—Patricia R.

People need to know that MPD is not an illness, but an obsolete survival tool. —Tony B.

When I was diagnosed, I wish someone would have explained to me that I was not crazy. I felt crazy, and still do at times. I did not really know what MPD meant, even though a calmness came from within as if to say "Someone knows we are here." I needed more validation. I wish I knew that there is no exact way a multiple should be. I wish I had felt better about describing my internal world. I wish someone would have told me that MPD was not "bad." —Susan C.

When we were first diagnosed as having MPD, on one hand, it was a relief to finally have the secret of the "others" out in the open. However, the diagnosis was also terrifying. We believed that MPD was crazy—that it was some kind of defective disease. Having that diagnosis applied to us was proof that we were evil and didn't deserve to be alive. What we've learned since that time and what we wish we had known then is that MPD is not crazy. Just the opposite. Becoming multiple was the healthiest reaction we could have had to the abusive situation we were in.

Another misconception we had about MPD was that all multiples are exactly the same. We believed that since we weren't like the multiples we had seen on TV or read about, we couldn't possibly be a multiple. We also thought that if we were multiple, we would have to become just like the sensationalized multiples. We have learned that all people are a product of their history—of their life. Since no two multiples had to survive exactly the same circumstances, people with MPD will experience and use their multiplicity uniquely. Simply put, just as no two people are the same, no two multiples could possibly be the same. It was a relief to find out that we didn't have to fit in a "box," bound up by a diagnosis. —Annette K.

"We" is "Me" reversed. Find it. —Toni R.

The thing I would have liked to have known most when I was first diagnosed as multiple is that MPD is not some horrible mental illness that people never recover from. My therapist tried to convey the message that recovery is possible, but I had a *great* deal of difficulty believing him. Craziness is one of my greatest fears and being told that I had many personalities living within me because of the atrocities I endured growing up was the most convincing evidence that I was crazy. I was afraid of my "people." I was afraid of what they would do, especially after reading some of the books that have been written.

I would like to have known some of the things that might happen: like my alters going places and then leaving me to come back, (not knowing where I am), or like little ones coming out at inopportune times. I have experienced my share of embarrassments and uncomfortable situations, but for the most part, my alters have pulled together and saved us from harm. —Terry J.

When I was first diagnosed as having MPD, I wish that I had known it was a creative way of staying alive, and that I am not alone with this diagnosis. It would also have been helpful to know that people are learning more about MPD as time goes on. Also, that I am still one person—an individual with rights just like anyone else—not a freak of nature. —Martha H.

I wished I had known that many (or most) multiples do not overtly show symptoms, like Sybil or Eve. I felt so "labeled": so categorized, so stigmatized, so isolated.

I wish I had known to expect five or more years of therapy to overcome MPD. Although it may have been overwhelming to know this at first, I might have dealt with therapy more realistically as a result.

I wish I had known that MPD is more common than once believed. I didn't want to feel so "unusual."

I wish I had known that my multiples were there because I *chose* to be that way (even if unconsciously). It took a long, long, *long* time to accept the parts for what they were, and to realize that they were part of me. —Lori B.

When I was first diagnosed with MPD, I appreciated learning a good definition, an explanation of the cause, and the reassurance that I was neither crazy nor alone. —Marcia L.

I wish I had realized that a diagnosis offers peace, understanding and hope. I knew what was going on in my mind and my life, but other people (friends and strangers) saw me differently. —Kathleen O.

At the time I was first diagnosed, I wish I had known that there were others like me and that I wasn't just "crazy." I wish that I had also known that there would eventually be help. Being labeled "hopeless," as I was by one institution, did not help my self-esteem. —Patsy Q.

As a multiple presently exchanging information with two other persons newly diagnosed with MPD, I am finding that the questions they asked are the same ones I wanted to ask when I first started treatment.

Here are my answers to those common questions:

Q) Am I a freak? a monster? the only one? crazy?

A) No, you are/were intelligent enough to develop a unique and extremely effective coping mechanism to survive as a child. There are many people like us, but all don't have the good fortune of being diagnosed and treated appropriately.

Q) Should I tell my family/relatives/friends/strangers?

A) Not until you are strong enough to face the possibility of rejection and/or ridicule. You will need a basic education in and a good working knowledge of the dynamics of MPD, so that you are prepared to answer questions. Some people will accept and understand, others will back up from fear, revulsion, lack of understanding.

Q) Am I different than I was before the diagnosis? Are weird things going to start happening around me?

A) You, as a system, are not different. You, as a group, have lived, survived and functioned for virtually your whole life. This diagnosis makes you *feel* differently about yourself, but you haven't changed. You may choose to change your lifestyle/habits/friends, etc., but your life won't change of its own volition. You are what you have always been.

Q) *Are the others really separate beings?*

A) Yes and no. Yes, in that alters have developed their own memories, feelings, opinions, habits, etc., and their own coping mechanisms. No, in that, in some sense, you all are one. When all the pieces are put together, you will feel like a whole being again.

Q) *But I don't ever remember anything really bad happening to me!*

A) Memories are often hidden inside. You don't need to contemplate every ill deed ever done to you, or try to force memory. It will all come as the system develops trust in the therapist, trust in itself, and strength. You'll have everything you need when the time is right. —Julie W.

When I was first diagnosed I wish I knew:

—that I did not need to feel so ashamed. MPD helped me survive into adulthood.

—that all the voices I had for so many years were real and coming from within me. For years I was so scared to share the fact that I heard voices inside my head. I thought I would be told I was crazy. It was another painful secret to keep and caused great anxiety.

—that I am not alone or a freak. I have met other people (men and women) with this disorder.

—that many more personalities would be emerging after my diagnosis. They feel safe to come out even though it scared some of us.

—that this diagnosis will not be understood by all people and to be *very, very* careful who I tell.

—Grace Rose

The Beginning

Will R.

I started life as *I*,
early on I became *we*
Abuse was a cause
Survival was a goal.
Others do not understand
Violence has been a part
that we're not proud of
just didn't know the way.
It took us a while to realize
that help could be found
to work at becoming *I* again
and maybe find happiness.
Remember God does understand
with very good reason
He's a multiple too,
The Father, Son and Holy Spirit.
Look at the world He has made
We can enjoy it also
Don't despair now
The end is in sight.

From the Outside

Susan P.

From the outside, people see just one;
but from the inside, we all see each other, just as we are . . .
. . . little girls gazing out curiously at colored leaves
        dancing and playing in patterns on the pavement . . .
. . . little boys bouncing along and balancing bravely
        with arms spread wide as we step along the street curb . . .
. . . grown-up girls glancing both ways to look for cars and,
        seeing none, allowing the balancing game to continue
        until gently guiding us across the street . . .
. . . grown-up boys, as committed protectors,
        escorting us past any and all potential dangers
        with sincere and genuine caring.

And this is how we are from the inside,
        all parts together,
        yet still our separate selves.

Little Girl Dream On

Annette K.

Unicorns and butterflies
Little girl dream on.
The world is beauty
through your eyes.
So please—
Teach me to see.

Death is not
The opposite of life
For to not live is evil
And evil is a binding force
No one—
Can go free.

My friend I want to live.

Unicorns and butterflies
Little girl dream on.
Your innocent laughter
Fills the sky.
So please—
Teach me to fly.

Demons and monsters

Are my world
They rape my mind
And soul
Without hope—
I tried to die.

My friend I want to live.

Unicorns and butterflies
Little girl dream on.
Your gentle touch
Brings warmth and peace.
So please—
Teach me to give.

Knives and fire
Fill my eyes
The tools of hate
And rage
I had my life—
But did not live.

My friend I want to live.

Unicorns and butterflies
Little girl dream on.
The gifts you share are kindness and
light.
So please—
Teach me to love.

Resolve

By Gregory B.

There is a box of 8mm color films that my mother coaxed my father into filming as I grew up. It was only on special occasions this cyclops rose from its box in the hall to devour anything sentimental to tender. They bought the camera with green stamps and the projector from a bonus. The films created sit unedited in a shoe box from Peralman's. They are individually boxed in orange, yellow and blue-green, smelling like dusty rotten cardboard. The films sit in the dark quietly unwinding in wait for another cyclops of light to burn through them. I pull them down and plug in their monster's tail. He's alive again. I shake the box. They rattle. I hear the slinky sound of my celluloid childhood rattle like old bones.

Old dried up pens have etched dates and birthdays on the boxes. They scribbled "Dad's Parents" or "Mom's Family." They are split in two rows, Greg-Christmas and Kyle-Christmas. I've never seen any of them. The projector is set up at one end of my mother's dining room and projects light all the way into the front room, filling the wall with bobbing pastel heads and birthday parties. Pancake ghosts fly within a square as big as a billboard but as thin as a thought. A world lands on the wall. So I sit next to this steaming monster and watch. I see my two-year-old eyes recorded by an awkward giant with a spotlight. I toddle giggling from one room to the next smiling in big white shoes and a bow tie. I think for a while, then the film is over.

As I start the machine again the wall melts into a three-year-old world of yellow pajamas with plastic feet and white snaps. A child walks around a Christmas tree with a big red cowboy hat and guns strapped to his chubby waist. It is me. I notice the huge brown eyes, high Indian cheekbones and bright blonde crew cut. I see the smile. It's mine too.

The screen jumps to our kitchen. I am six feet high and scooting a little red stool across the room to reach a phone as big as an icebox. The lights from the camera get too close to my eyes and I squint and run into a chair. I laugh and my lips move in the silence—"D A D D Y."

I stop the film and role it back. I play it again then rewind. It plays again. I smile as I watch down from heaven on a family and its baby. I see them smile, and they argue about this thing and then something else. The film ends and Christmas 1964 is over again. The room is dark and the face of a three-year-old is burned in my eyes. This is me before.

I rewind the film and put on another. It starts with a blur of bright orange, the sun I think. It is my third grade summer. I recognize the short sleeve plaid shirt and rolled up straight legged jeans. I am running around our backyard, starting then stopping behind a mimosa tree that is now as big as the house. I stop and see a neighbor, the film still rolling. I see my parents talk to them. I stand in the background of this silent film watching. Film rolling. My dog runs to the fence, everyone smiles and waves. No sound. I stand there listening in the distance, they laugh. The film ends.

I rewind it and play it again and again. I freeze the frames. I fast forward. I stop. It starts again. The images begin to fill something within me and take something away. My chest grows warm and I taste the salt of my tears. I go limp and slide to the floor. From there I try to see into a child's eyes as big as a wall, but the boy doesn't stare back. I start to touch his face but the moving picture blurs and then bursts into white as the film ends again.

This is me after.

I have always wondered what I was like then, and wondered too what I would be like if the sexual abuse hadn't happened. I've always wondered if I would be taller, if I would be stronger, if I would be more like Wally Cleaver.

I can remember being in a lumberyard and seeing a boy like I would have been. Like I could have been, might have been. I see him talk, and smile. I am proud of him. He stands behind his father. I smile to myself, and I die a little bit never knowing.

The smell of burning dust and heat from the projector catch me and pull me back to the dining room. I roll up the films and put them back into the box in two separate rows. I put them back in the closet and wait for the projector to cool.

In the same closet is a book of photos, black and white, birthdays and Christmas. I open them and take one photo out, slip it in my pocket to frame for my desk.

That is where it is now. A little boy in track shoes looks out and smiles with eyes of trust and hope and vulnerability. He calls me to remember and to be proud. To remember warm September summers with squeals of delight and to be proud that even in survival there can be the vulnerability to trust again.

Silent Screams ·

Peggy J.

we tried to tell you
in so many ways,
the pain, fear, despair, shame;
yet what came forth were
the silent screams.

it's not that we haven't tried—
you and us—to speak,
to hear, to understand,
to listen to these
silent screams.

there's no dramatics, no drama
no hysterics, no acting
yet we plead for help through
the silent screams.

we're screaming now;
please hear us, please hold us,
please reach out even though we look so calm;
please don't let these be more of
those silent screams.

We Are All Very Hungry For Life

Kathy A.

How fleeting the lightness of my Spirit is.
How heavy and endless are the Dark Moments, How long they seem to
    linger.
Always to be lurking close by, Threatening. Waiting in every innocent
    Shadow.
I run by joyful in movement, in spirit, unsuspecting of their presence.
Momentarily lulled into a sense of peace, of security and they Grab.
And because I was not watching I am drawn tightly within their grasp.
What to Do?
Do I exchange the fleeting moments of light free footsteps
to be ever lost in caution and watchfulness
Never to know the World or her Bounty
No. . . . I must Risk and run into the Peace and Freedom if for only a
    moment.
For I am, We are, so Hungry!

Becoming Aware

Judy W.

Now I see them
Now I don't
apart
together
pieces
whole
an internal uproar
a rush of each one
followed by the next.
It's quiet
are they gone?
or are they gone until
I see them again?

The Promise Of Love

Marcia L.

Am I afraid to die?
    Not I.
    I died
and there was peace and release.

What I fear is living,
    to look back over my life and grieve
        What could have been.
        What should have been.
    To look ahead and hope for what
        has been promised me.

I thought I was given a choice to feel pain or not to feel
    so I chose not to feel.
I didn't know there was another choice
    a choice to feel love.
I never experienced feeling loved
    so by choosing not to feel
        I do not feel love.

The wall that protects me from the pain
    also keeps me from feeling the love
    that should pass through the wall and
    into others.

Breaking down the wall also allows—
    all the pain—
    What a price to pay for love.

Love that is only a hope is only a promise.
No one could give the promise I wanted.
    I was afraid to hope, to want
        I didn't hope
        I didn't want
        I was safe

I couldn't be hurt or betrayed.
I wanted nothing
I hoped for nothing.

I'm not completely free from pain
        because these are holes in my wall
        my children are there.
So do I tear down the wall or fix the wall
One allows me to be alive
the other allows me to live and love
        . . . or so they say.

Faces

Kathleen P.

Peeking around
the corners of my
mind.

Hiding
from one
another.

Afraid
to get too close
Afraid
to go too far.

Within And Without

Kathleen P.

One body
cannot contain the dreamgirls

wobbly wooden dolls
within dolls

We echo ancient grievances
dissolve

then reappear
every one untouchable

nerve curlers
without bones or mother blood

Polish the surface
to a lucent sheen

we remain indelible
the inevitability of morning

the persistence of night.

Genesis

Diana D.

Of Diana was born
"Lynn"
& of "Lynn"
"Jenny"
& many more
to come
Delivered out of pain
Contractions induced
No anesthetic
No mid-wife
to hold a hand
to encourage
to strengthen
With each birth
came
the anesthesia

the one
to hold a hand
to encourage
to strengthen
to protect

A woman squats in a field
delivers
straps the new one on
keeps working
no one notices
save herself
Later it will cry out its need
but never she her own

The Children

Charlene R.

Do You Know Where Your Children Are?

No.
How could I?
I couldn't protect them
I wasn't there.

SAD—she's torn and battered
Poor Child—first it was just touch
Then came pain and tearing . . . there was
Blood.
She learned to leave
To make the quantum leap.
The next god to take SAD was the
New grandmother
And she attacked the other senses
With screaming and curses.
And then beatings.
SAD learned not to duck or cry out
It got worse if she did.
And then one day
She disappeared.
Did she feel that she would die if she stayed?

Dear IMP
I don't know when you came along
I've just acknowledged you.
But someone had to be there
To fill in the empty space.
Class clown
Silly funny child
Endearing child
Oh IMP, you make me laugh!

There are others
Standing in the shadows.
One would have to be
KNOWING.
You are the woman-child.
It's all right to stay there
For now.
You don't have to be ashamed.
You did what you had to do
To stay.
Each time you pushed SAD out of the way
You were keeping her from dying.

Who is hiding
Behind SAD?
I've seen you in

Dreams
And brief memories,
Like flashes of
Lightning.

Are you the POTATO CHILD?
The one who whimpers
But cannot sob.

Many Of One

By "All of Me" and the A-Team

Hi. My name has many, so many am I. I am a lady, but yet I am a man. I am an adult, yet I am a child. I am meek, yet I am bold. I have many talents and speak in many different voices, yet I am one. I have many in my family, big and small, yet I have none.

I can be many things at one time. I can be happy, but then be sad. Or I can be fun and then afraid. I like to be at peace with myself, and yet I am only a piece of myself. I can remember almost everything but yet I forget all things. I have pain, but yet feel none at all. My thoughts are many, yet I hold only a few. My eyes see many things, yet my mind holds illusions.

I am old enough to think, yet too young to know. I can travel many places, yet I never leave the room. I can always see yesterday, and never remember today. I am big, but yet I am small. I am old, but no, I am young. I am me, yet I still become you. I have a lot of love, yet I hate. I have many friends, and young ones to play with, yet I am still alone. I talk to many people, and they talk to me, yet I talk not at all.

I hold a lot of dreams, and yet the dreams still hold me. I have a lot of ideas, and many fantasies too, yet I know them not at all. I can see and know what is real, yet I am in a fairy tale. I can talk of many things, yet I keep a "secret." I have but one life, yet I live many.

You know me, yet I know not you. You see the good, but I know the bad. You see the laughter, while I am sad. I hear many voices, yet there's no one around. I know not my faith, yet I have hope. I am all things, yet I am none. I can see and feel the sun, but I still walk in darkness. I can say one thing, but mean many. I hear the cries, yet you hear the birds. I know of things, yet not of life.

I know of people, but not as friends. So when you see me (yet I don't see you), speak to me as many. And many will speak to you.

Changes

By Kate W.

I used to think of myself as evil. I imagined that my skin was dissolvable, a kind of "film" that could blow away in a breath. I mean this literally. I experienced it literally. For example, if I spoke too softly and the other person failed to respond, I'd think, "Oh no, I'm gone."

At the center of myself, I pictured something dark and slimy there where a soul should be. I was afraid of x-rays, pap smears, sex . . . because someone else might see that thing or get hurt by that thing. I was afraid that I smelled bad, and on certain days I'd be so embarrassed by the smell that I'd stay in the house.

I was nauseated a lot of the time . . . not in my intestines but in my mind. It was existential dizziness . . . existing on and off. And my head would hurt, in therapy, silent screaming headaches that would try to shut me off, shut me up.

I've been in therapy for two and a half years, and I've stopped smelling bad. I breathe in and there's air with perfume in it . . . or grass maybe, or soap. My therapist and I reinforce the skin . . . she describes it and I believe it. We create a substance around me. There is pain, clarity, grief. We put the fear back in time, we make characters smaller, I hold on. The anger remains illusive, or "minor," but I know it's there. I can't use utensils, we figured out, because I'm afraid of hurting somebody. (I'll just pretend I'm Bohemian for the time being.)

I don't think there's a creature inside my body anymore, a "thing." I know that my body is filled with natural *human* stuff: tissue, water, blood. And I extend all the way out to the inside of my skin . . . that won't disappear.

Maybe most importantly, as far as change goes, I don't blame myself for having "mind sets" anymore. It was a survival mechanism. My struggle now is to dismantle the war machine, now that the war is over.

Calvin Tells It Like It Is

By MaryLou J.

I am Calvin, one of the forty-three alters of MaryLou who has Multiple Personality Disorder. My intention is to take you inside our system, our world, and explain the pleasures and pains of our existence.

Some laymen would call us "fictional," made up by a bored individual, but that is not how we see it.

Take a look: I am forty-five years old and have been ML's father figure for many years. My interests and tastes are my own. For example, I prefer classical music, play the piano, read voraciously, and frown upon silly behavior.

Around me are many different and unusual personalities. Some are whole and have serious and important functions; others are merely fragments who perform minor functions. All of us have names, ages, ideas, and opinions. We discuss events among ourselves and work to keep the body we belong to safe, healthy and intact.

How do we decide which alter comes out? It is quite simple, though it can be complex due to vanity or rivalry among us. The presenting personality is either the one most adept at handling the current situation, or one who wants or needs to express something. Some of the younger ones pop out playfully, wanting attention.

Our system is made up of MaryLou, the birth personality, and of adults, teenagers, children—both genders. We have the Helper who aids us in our coming and going and who can scan the system and spot the problem at hand then suggest corrections.

One of us eats food: a healthy, low calorie, low fat diet. MaryLou has embarked on a fitness program to keep our shelter strong and well. The body is important to us and must be always protected.

Like all people, alters have quirks and peculiarities. Not one of us presents a perfect front. We are created from crisis in ML's childhood and adolescence and formed into individuals who have specific reasons to function.

ML has only recently become aware of us. She has a history of blackouts, which were the times when we were coming forth in her place. Her first impression was distress, suicidal ideations and anger.

Through therapy and medication, ML survived, as did we. She now understands how six years of sexual abuse and the subsequent insecurity

23

created her forty-three personalities. She knows it is one body, and one mind; however, she cannot think of us as being her own creations. ML comes to us for advice, suggestions, and socializing. Also, she has learned to rest inside while others of us function for her.

Not only do we tend to our functions, we also take time to pursue our individual interests. The younger ones come out to draw, play, or color. Others of us read, take walks, talk to friends, listen to music, do crafts, etc. We are like a mass yet we are separate.

Integration, which some of us resist, lies ahead. It will be a long and difficult struggle and ML will be whole again. I, Calvin Quincy J_____ will be part of that one personality, but I will remain an individual always in these words I write. The swift strokes of a pen capture me so that someone else may learn of me.

Multiple Personality Disorder is curable, but only by hard work, sacrifice and patience.

What do I feel about that?

All systems "GO"!

It is both terrifying and humiliating to discuss these experiences. Forgetting so much is embarrassing, not to mention confusing and frightening. It is often difficult to convey experiences because of memory lapses, so I hope therapists get neither frustrated nor angry with their patients. But, most of all, I would like therapists (and others) to know that multiples are sensitive people with feelings just like anyone else. —Martha H.

If only people knew how much in the dark I feel when being told about things I do or say when I'm not "me" . . . how much I'm *unaware* of behavior changes. For me, MPD is like having all the company you can stand in your life. It's not knowing how to dress or act in public. —Amie R.

Think about the last time you forgot someone's name or a minor detail. Did trying to remember drive you nuts? MPD is like that, but there are many, many more things you don't remember. Add to that the fact that you forget that you don't remember, or that when you do finally remember, you FORGET that you remembered, etc. No wonder we are confused, give incomplete and/or inconsistent life histories, don't remember what went on in the earlier part of the therapy session or from one session to another. No wonder we can't track progress and we get discouraged with the whole process.

MPD therapy is not like losing weight, where you can see the progress in a measurable way. —Patricia M.

How does it *FEEL* to be MPD? It feels ugly, dirty and repulsive. It feels like being the elephant man. Who would ever want to hold a thing like you or love such a deformed creature? Dying would feel better.

You scream and guess what? No one notices anything. You make jokes when your guts are hemorrhaging and guess what? No one notices anything. Your stomach lurches and your bowels loosen because you can't find the answer to that easy question your therapist just asked and guess what? He doesn't even notice the beads of sweat on your lip. —Wendy W.

The experience of MPD is HELL. We are a good group in that we are kind to those inside and out yet we feel so often unworthy, unlovable because of our experiences. We wouldn't wish this on anyone. We work hard at not acting out, but instead, we try to talk and say how we feel. The difficulty to represent so many at one time is confusing to me and to those who hear me. To appear "whole" like everyone else, yet to have my thinking and feelings so influenced by others (inside) is often uncomfortable.

It is as difficult for me to imagine being "whole" as it is for a whole person to imagine being fragmented. —Susan C.

Inner Life

Jo Anne M.

Very silent sighs. Groans, quiet and alone.
I hate my life, my separation from the world, from God.
So ashamed am I that I isolate myself even in a crowd—
silence, the quiet that pierces my ears with the sound of its thunder and
    gorges my
heart with its fierce bolt of lightning.
Never a moment's peace, never a moment's rest . . .
Never, never a stillness in my heart.

The experience of MPD seemed normal to me. I thought everybody experienced life just like I did. I was troubled and confused, depressed at times, but so many people are. It was a relief to find out life could be more coherent, but because I had no memory of any abuse, I really believed I had lied to my therapist, made it up. After my diagnosis, life became clearer, and more confusing all at once.

My counselor had experience with other MPD people and was rock solid, patient and kind. She helped me see that I am O.K. But I must accept that the way I experience the world has been shaped by abuse. The fragmentation served a purpose, but now as an adult I can decide if the purpose of fragmentation serves me. Do I need that protection? At first I did. Now I don't. But I needed to grow to that place. —Cynthia S.

Minute by Minute

By Brenda E.

Turmoil seems around every corner. Is there a way to escape it? I think not. We live with fear every day. Do not tell us to think positive. The word has little or no meaning to us now. We are just trying to survive.

Can you grasp the need for minute-to-minute survival? I wonder. You all sit in your cozy little chairs in your quiet little minds and wonder what to eat for the day. We, on the other hand, sit in tension all of the time, wondering if now is the time we will go over the edge. Do you sit and look around every little corner to see if that one person is lurking there?

Certainly not. People would think you crazy. But what if that lurking person lived inside of you? What if he or she had the force to destroy you and all that you know and love? Could you sit in your comfy little chair and not worry? I wonder, and yet that is just what you expect all of us to do.

Weariness is a part of every day. The ones on the inside grow stronger. You tell us to fight. What if there is no fight left? Can you not understand weariness? Can you not understand fear for one's self or sanity? No, these things are far from your imagination. But let me tell you these are what we live with every day.

Hope, you say. Have "hope." The word sounds wonderful. We'll try, but remember please, our war never stops. Some of our people never sleep. They thrive on fear. Our fear especially.

Please do not judge, you have not been in our place. You cannot begin to understand the daily fight that must be fought. Don't tell me that we are strong enough to fight, we are weary. Don't look at us and say pull yourself together. Our System doesn't work that way.

Don't look at us and say you understand. You can't, you have never fought this battle. Don't tell us to think positive or think of us as one others do not understand. PLEASE, PLEASE, try to see that we are all working the best that we can. We do not try to live your life for you, please do not try to live ours. You cannot, because we have enough trouble living our own.

We have others who will try to make your life run more smoothly, but even they tire and must pull back. Please try to realize we want this to be over as much as you do. Our life is not our own, it belongs to many others and so we must do the best we can with the things that are given to us. Most of us realize that it puts a strain on your life and we are sorry, but look at our life, if you can call it that. The anger, terror, fear and weariness abound. Can we control this much longer without rest? We'll see!

Simply Whole

By Judith D.

> They say that the soul will survive
> But we want more than just to survive
> We seek life with the simplicity of wholeness.
> And so follows an explanation of how we were found;

and the key to unlocking us all from the closets of hell to find ourselves, trying to come back to the normalcy of life as others know it, as we have never known it to be.

Throughout the years they've tried to silence our world. They've used drugs and shock treatments but it had never altered our world; the only result is that some of us have died. After years of everyone trying to silence us, I have learned to answer the question differently. Everyone's favorite question, "Do you hear voices?" I would look at them and think, "Why do they ask us? Everyone does." I never realized that everyone's world was not like ours. The answer to the question is yes; it is what we call our world—the world we live in—that we survive in.

Two years ago we were gang raped; and although we knew things had changed that night, it was to be the beginning of the decline into a world of madness. Please, let me descend into madness. We endured silence for six more months. But silencing the pain could now cost the body in which we live its life. Once again we entered the hospital to be saved, but the pain and sadness were so great we would not let anyone in. But things around us would change even if we did not want them to. The doctor of many years could not deal with the rape, so he called in someone else. We knew the ugliness inside would push people away if they knew and what he did reinforced that feeling inside. We knew that we were dirty.

This woman came and met me in the hospital. The "voices" said caution, or she will walk away. But she was different. She knew the dirtiness we felt, and after many weeks she asked about the "voices"—it always comes back to that question. She asked about the headaches, and all the time I lost in a day. She asked me if the voices had names. I looked with surprise; in thirty-four years, no one had ever asked that question. Jennifer said to tell her; she felt safe, and so I began to try to explain our world; but the pain and panic took over. And so, we were to embark on another change. She told us we didn't have to stay with the doctor of many years. We could look for someone else, and we did.

I started to see a new therapist. She asked so many questions, and there was always the question from her, "Why?" The more she tries to understand our world, the more panic we feel. Then one week she told me she felt my diagnosis was incorrect. She told me that based on the symptoms, tests, and interviews with me, she felt I was multiple. The fear inside clutched my heart and soul. Please, let me be schizophrenic. Please, don't take that away from us. It is what we need to hide behind. Please, she has to be wrong. But she wasn't wrong. She had acquired a key to this world of ours. The children inside now trust her with who they are; and at times, I'm jealous of the easiness with which they speak with her. But there are still many times I want with all my heart to go back and hide behind being schizophrenic. It didn't hurt and there were no expectations to change in the world of Schizophrenia. But the door to our world has been unlocked. As days have become weeks and weeks have become months, my need for the old diagnosis has diminished. It has been with me over thirty years. It's like saying good-bye to an old friend.

Feelings are new. Pain is deep. I was warned before embarking on this trip that it may be a trip through hell. The screams that have never been heard, someday will be heard. The pain that has always been numbed will surface and someday the rage will spill out and again she will help me pick up the pieces.

And now as I begin this journey of getting to know those pieces, and putting the puzzle together, I know that we have a chance to realize our full potential. But the most important thing is that we see ourselves as being sane. It is the first time in thirty-four years that our picture of ourselves is one of sanity. At times, when the memories and pain get too great, we still retreat into our world. But slowly as we re-emerge we learn how to see the world from others' eyes and learn to see the newness as a beginning.

And so we know the soul inside has survived

And so we are working hard to survive

With everyone working together, we will find the simplicity that was taken away as a child, and bring it to live with us in the present. Unlike the hell in which we grew up, this hellish journey we have chosen has a purpose. The purpose is to make us whole. To see life as a flower opening in the warmth of the sun—to us, that is simplicity.

There are over 35 of us and we are in the early stages of recovery. It's torture much of the time but each moment of freedom and togetherness makes the pain-filled times bearable. —Kathy A.

My mind seems like an old wooden Coke case, each bottle in its space, each full, each labeled. As I uncap each bottle and begin to empty it, I feel more freedom. The pain is enormous as the information spills into my conscious mind. One day, all the bottles will be empty and the divisions can be removed. I will have memories like everyone else, yet like no one else's.

My soul hurts; it is in great pain. It is as if there is a cancer there that no one sees. I look fine. The hurt and pain are there, hiding, but no longer secret.

Is this because I am a multiple or because of abuse—abuse that eats at the fiber of oneself, the abuse that causes all those Coke cases to fill with bottles, and the bottles with liquid, neatly named and divided? —Sarah F.

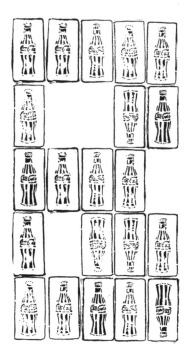

Roads, Trails, Missing Links

Marti P.

Back in time
off I go
To a time of decisions
I have made
to the fork in the road;
all of a sudden
my mind goes blank!
What happened here?
Where do I start?
Where do I end?
There must be a trail
in this mind of mine
Damn it!
It's disappeared again
Oh! There's a trail over here
Where will it lead
to where I must go
A little further
Around the bend
I can see the end
Damn it!
It's disappeared again
There's a trail over here!
Maybe it will lead me to
where I need to go
A little further!
Around the bend!
Can I see the end?
NO!
Here we go again
Another tangled mass
The trail, the road
it's invisible again

Will this tangled mass of
disappearing
    trails
        roads
            ever end!
I sure hope so
For beneath it all
I am sure is the
Key
    to
        finding
          me!

At the beginning, I wish I'd known how to handle the headaches. Do they ever end? Why didn't others see the MPD sooner?

What do other MPDs do about lost time? Do they make lists like me, or place cards at bedside to know what they must do each day?
—Nancy G.

When I was first diagnosed as MPD, I wish I had known how long the process of recovery was. I also wish someone had told me that I could expect more personalities to appear besides the ones I already knew. I also wish I was told that accepting a diagnosis of MPD was traumatic in itself.
—Marsha C.

Right from the start, I wanted somebody to tell me:
—How did we get to be an MPD? (How the hell did this happen?)
—Is it hopeless? Will one of the alters hurt and/or kill us or someone else, such as the person(s) who abused us?
—How many of us are there now and how many retired alters (from the past)? What are their names? How old are they? What do they look like? What do they do? Are they humans, animals, toys, plants? Do they speak English? Where do they live?
—How can we get rid of all of them? What is left after we do?
—Why are some alters animals, toys or plants?
—Why are all the feelings so hidden inside that they can't get out? Why can't we cry or get angry, etc.?
—Is it all my fault? —MaryLou P.

Sometimes I wonder:
How could we go unnoticed for so long, having different "parts"?
Am I ever going to be *one* person?
Why isn't it called . . . Multiple Personality *Response* instead of being a "disorder"? —Amie R.

My initial reaction to being diagnosed with MPD was a feeling of utmost anxiety about lack of control. My greatest fear, which grew as various personalities felt freer and more able to come and go, was the lack of control I *believed* that I had over my life. It took a long time for me to "hear" or possibly to "understand" that the diagnosis was actually a key to asserting control. Quite naturally, I had no real concept of "teamwork" and therefore, was not able to conceptualize it working among my vari-

33

ous personalities. This was something that I seemed to learn one situation at a time. When the bigger picture finally was revealed to me, everything got easier. —Carol T.

When I was first diagnosed with MPD, I wish that I had known the hard work that was involved. I wish that I had known that people knew so little about it and that they would be afraid and even cruel to me. I wanted to know nothing and yet everything about the cause. I was both embarrassed and glad that someone finally gave it a name. Someone would understand me and proceed to help me in learning about myself. —Linda B.

I basically knew I was MPD before I was diagnosed. I wish I had known how terrifying the memories are when they come back, and that the person who is recalling the memory still feels the fear as they did in the past. I would like to have known that we are divided for special reasons and that we are all going to be ok. —RC

If I had known what the general pattern was for people diagnosed with MPD, I don't believe I would have taken such stressful, high-management, high-profile positions where any aberration from "normal" behavior was cause for such embarrassment when noticed by political groups, entire staffs and the public. I have lost three jobs because of "multiple" behavior.

I again wish I had known earlier why sex was only "good" with someone I didn't love; why I couldn't ask for help under *any* circumstances, especially of a doctor or policeman; why I was terrified of snakes, the dark and fire; why I felt guilty all the time and why I felt like a "freak." I am glad I didn't know what a long, lonely journey it would be or I don't think I could have gone on. —Anne M.

I wish I had known originally that MPD cases are as individual as fingerprints. Even though I knew all people are different, I didn't entirely understand the wide variety of presentations of MPD. I would read books and journal articles looking for some markers for my own progress and I now know that isn't necessarily helpful. But my education about MPD, which I received as a result, has benefitted my therapy. —Alice O.

Searching for Answers

By Vickie G.

When I think of all the cracks I slipped through over the years trying to get help, an anger stirs inside me. It took so long before someone finally knew what I was suffering from!

For six years I had gone to several therapists, psychiatrists, even two pastors for help. Every time I complained of fatigue, headaches, panic episodes, visual disturbances, forgetfulness, memory problems, nightmares, fear, paranoia, etc., I would be told I was experiencing depression, anxiety, stress, hormone imbalance, PMS, post-partum blues, exhaustion, etc. Sometimes I was told I needed exercise, to slow down, blood work, *or* I would even be advised to pray more, read certain books, to lay my "burdens" down before God and ask protection against the strongholds of Satan! All my complaints were usually explained away as being symptomatic of depression.

I kept asking *why* I continued to get depressed and have nightmares? What was the reason?

Never were there real answers. I was given prescriptions (and scripture) to alleviate my symptoms, without uncovering the root cause. As time wore on, I felt less than a person, humiliated and frustrated because I couldn't gain any control over my life.

It was only after experiencing "flashbacks" a couple years ago, after being raped in my home, that I looked for new avenues of help. I began a process of discovering the horrors of a lost childhood.

After joining a group for incest survivors, an intense anxiety kicked in, and I found myself having more memory lapses. There was a disconcerting sense that something was terribly wrong or different about me. As I talked with other "group" members, I learned that we were all dissociating to a degree. What I didn't know was, I had been dissociating *severely* all my life.

When some new nightmares began and my sense of panic and confusion increased, I finally had to switch (for the last time) to a female therapist in hopes that I might be better understood and listened to. My new therapist had been my support group facilitator so she already knew some of my past and was willing to work with me on an individual basis.

My internal war raged, symptoms exacerbated, and I soon found myself hysterical and scared. The voices that I had heard before were now telling me to kill myself, and I was feeling crazier than ever. But the fear that gripped me was so frightening, I had to call my therapist and let her know all the strange things that I lacked the courage to admit before. That day, I lifted the phone, tears flooding my face, heart pounding, and I made contact with the only person I thought I could risk telling about the "voices." My hands were shaking and a voice mocked me, calling me "shithead." When I finally told her on the phone how suicidal and crazy I felt, she calmly assured me in her gentle voice that what I was going through was *not* crazy. We then began some serious exploration those next few weeks. Never did I ever think I could be multiple. When I finally learned I had MPD, I was dazed, but things slowly began to make sense.

If I had known about MPD when I was first diagnosed, maybe I wouldn't have felt so scared that my life might always be out of control, or that I might be "terminal"! There *is* hope. MPD is treatable!

I wish I'd known the difference between MPD and Schizo-Affective Disorder. I was misdiagnosed for four years. My mother had been diagnosed Paranoid Schizophrenic. —Kim B.

When I was first diagnosed with MPD, I couldn't believe it. The therapist that I was seeing felt he didn't know enough about MPD to treat me. He was able to make the diagnosis, but not to treat what he had diagnosed. So I got passed on.

I wish I had known another multiple. I wish my therapist had known more about MPD. I wish I'd had a better support system. —Diane H.

I wish I knew for sure that I could recover the memories needed for healing, and that I could survive in all ways until I got to a better place. —Barbara H.

Therapy is no piece of cake. It is the hardest work I have ever had to do. Sometimes I get the feeling that people just think I go four times a week to the therapist and we sit and chat about everyday problems. I wish it were that easy. —Diane H.

It is very hard to trust people. It is hard to believe people care. It is hard to let people in. And when you do start to trust somebody (your therapist), it's hard to keep on trusting them. I watch everybody all the time. I can love them a little bit, as long as they don't find out. —Judy S.

Healing from MPD is like putting a puzzle together without seeing the picture on the box. —Amie R.

Often, time spent in the therapist's office each week is the only time we feel safe and ok about being MPD.—Kathleen O.

TEARS....

heal the bleeding soul
cause huge headaches
open unhealed wounds
release unwanted pressure
are like heavy rain in a thunderstorm
are quiet
are lonely
are inviting
are isolating
just are.
—Toni R.

Therapy—The Early (Painful) Days

By Pamela F.

Having only recently been diagnosed as MPD, we find we have many more questions than answers.

Our therapist had suspected we were MPD, but we did not believe him. Then about two months ago, under hypnosis, he talked to one of the voices. It was very strange to hear Samantha talk out loud.

37

The next four days until we returned to therapy were horrible. Suddenly the voices went from inside to showing their separate identities. They were jealous that Samantha had gotten attention in her own therapy session; they wanted to be heard too. By the time we returned to see our therapist, ten of them wanted to have a turn.

We have introduced nineteen voices, each with its own story, its own pain, and its own needs.

How do we go on from here? We feel so broken apart.

How can we face the pain again? It seems impossible to relive it.

How do we function? Are we crazy?

What are we doing to our children, our family?

Right now there is no direction that is safe. Looking back means seeing and reliving the pain and suffering. Looking forward is filled with uncertainty.

Now all we can do is live for each therapy session, in the hope that whomever needs help that day can get it. In the days between our appointments, we fight over who is up next. Or whomever had a turn at our last session flaunts the attention they received for all to see.

They are all so needy, so full of pain and anger.

We thought everyone lived with these voices, but thankfully for them, they don't.

Some days it is like WW III going on inside. They battle with words and pain and replaying scenes from our past. They are brutal in their attacks. They know where to hit and how to hurt. Our therapist is kind and patient with each of the ones he has met so far. He talks of a time when the others will have worked through their pain and have grown up.

To us it seems like an impossible dream and sometimes we picture him as our Don Quixote, off fighting the windmills in our lives.

We don't know how we would make it through without having him intercede in the battles, calm the combatants and try to listen, for just a little while, to whomever is hurting the most that day.

Hypnosis is a miracle he uses to get in touch with the others, just one at a time. It is amazing, when he talks to them under hypnosis. No one interrupts. No one screams "Don't tell him that! He will hate you if you tell him that."

We hear those words so often. There is so much fear that we will do something that will make him go away.

Does everyone with MPD feel that way?

We want so much to always do the right thing, so he will be there to help us. We need him so much that it is scary. We feel so vulnerable right now.

Will the fear ever go away? What will happen to us? Will we ever come together?

We have been apart for so long. How could parts that hurt and hate so much ever unite? How do we learn that we don't have to be afraid of our therapist going away before it is right for us to live? How do we know what is right and what is wrong?

Pick any subject. Among them, the others' opinions will span the spectrum of thought.

Our son is in therapy, too. We look to his therapist to provide some sense of normalcy and stability in his life. His therapist tells us to find the one who can best parent and let that one be in charge of his care.

How do we tell? Some days the others flip in and out of control. It must be very difficult for him.

We don't know what the future holds. At this point we can only take it one day at a time. Although we would like to be whole someday, for now we can only hope that our outward functionality hides our inner turmoil.

Therapists should talk to multiples and learn what has helped them in previous therapy. Don't diagnose too quickly, and don't shove the MPD label down their throats. Don't expect the person to switch on demand or for every self to have a name. Multiples are *all* different and do things differently. We are *unique*, with unique pasts, and we have very special positive and negative selves among us.

You couldn't begin to understand the relief I feel to have finally found a therapist who knows what has been going on in my life and who gives of her time and energy to help me try to put my pain to rest.
—Catherine H.

It was my host's wish to first discover if there were other MPDs within his region. He wished to contact other MPDs with whom he could speak at length with regards to overcoming MPD and addressing the buried, traumatic infrastructure upon which his multiplicity was built. The host further wished to know the mean length of time required to bring about an integrated whole.

With regards to my own personal interests, I wished to discover whether or not it would be possible to remove the more malevolent alternates. I have found published material regarding this issue sadly lacking in both depth and substance. My existence has been analogous to that of a breeder reactor containment coordinator with regards to one particularly malevolent alternate. I attempted many times to eradicate and/or render harmless this most unpredictable and uncontrollable alternate. These attempts met with little measurable success. —J. Robert

I wish I had known how expensive it is to get well. It is difficult to have to decide whether to go to therapy or buy food.

I wish I had known that developing MPD was a normal response to trauma; that being able to leave my body allowed me to endure the abuse. I compared myself to Hollywood-type MPD and denied having the condition because I was not/am not flamboyant. —Anne C.

Tell us, are we MPD or are the psychics correct? They adamantly claim that we are simply having "out of body experiences," which are normal. We experience "astro-flighting," which is a "phenomenal plus" because we can visit our past lives and grow from those past experiences. Are the automatic writings and the products of our artistic and creative abilities indicative of others possessing our body? Could it be that we have achieved a higher level in this human race? —Barbara G.

Pick a Number

By Barbara G.

For as long as we can remember, we have seen an array of doctors as well as nine different therapists. Our description of difficulties remained the same, *only the diagnosis differed among the professionals!*

We have been diagnosed and treated with medication *and* hospitalizations for: (1) migraine headaches, (2) Manic Depression, (3) Bipolar Depression, (4) insomnia, (5) Temporal Lobe Epilepsy, (6) Borderline Personality Disorder, (7) Schizophrenia, (8) Schizoid Personality Disorder, (9) thyroid dysfunction, (10) sexual disorders, (11) Dyslexia, (12) Seasonal Affective Disorder, (13) hysteria, (14) feigning paralysis,

(15) uncontrolled sleepwalking, (16) Cyclothymia, (17) neurosis, (18) psychosis, (19) amnesia, (20) hearing disabilities, (21) heart problems, (22) various degrees of visual impairment, including blindness, (23) blackouts, (24) suicidal attempts, etc., etc., etc.

So when you ask, "What do you wish you knew about MPD when you were first diagnosed?" CHILL OUT! What we really want to know is: IS THIS REALLY MPD OR IS IT ANOTHER ATTEMPT ON YOUR PART TO STRING US ALONG?! Soon we will be the entire DSM-III-R. As our dear friend, a respected young deaf dentist, jokes (with meaning): "Well, it certainly is interesting! And it's a bonus to have so many talented friends."

MPD is not contagious and NOT the result of talking to stuffed animals.
—Tony B.

A View from the Inside Out

By Peggy J.

Let's take a journey into a structure, a particular human structure with the label of Multiple Personality Disorder (MPD). Outside appearances indicate normality and don't make much difference. She can be short/tall, thin/fat, or pretty/plain. Personally, she can be a winner one minute, a pain the next; gentle first, violent next—and all without any warning. Her unpredictability drives others up the wall and they walk away.

Instead, let's walk inside.

It really doesn't matter what it took for this person to be a "multiple," but please know that it wasn't an occasional slap in the face or periodic yelling. The terror, trauma, horror, or whatever word you choose, that comprises her past is unique to her and still generic to all "multiples."

Looking through her eyes is strange—seeing scenes superimposed upon each other or watching a body that looks like hers doing things she is ashamed of. Even more confusing is hearing the statements of others that she slapped someone; or screwed with some person she doesn't even know; and on and on. She hears you say that she beat her kids but she knows that she would die stopping anyone from hurting her kids—including herself.

She wanders around in a world of many people, but sees her body as the only one present. She hears the cries of children within her begging for help; of others threatening harm to the children within, to her, and to those outside her. You think she's a snob because she doesn't participate in group activities or isolates herself, when being in a crowd only confuses her more because of the "crowd" within. And sometimes she chooses isolation only to protect herself and you from another incident that she may not remember.

She knows that somewhere within her there IS sanity, but can only find craziness. Sometimes she dares to look around to remember—the last hour, day, week, even year and all there is, is blackness; and yet she knows she did exist during that time—she is alive, isn't she? You tell her what she did during those times saying, "she was a joy, a baby, a jack-ass, a whore," all that and more. She'll tell you "no" and call you a liar, a pain, a problem.

One part of her will know, or better said, "sense" that something has indeed happened and the best she can do is wait for the hand to slap, razor to slash, foot to kick, or fist to fly. Sometimes she runs away because she just can't take the wait and pain any longer.

Despite all that, somewhere deep, deep inside she wants to be better and is willing to do whatever it takes to be better. She'll give you her heart and soul; bared, exposed, beaten—if telling the past and present will bring peace. She'll do most anything you ask, if only to be better. And when she sees the festering cancer of MPD growing and killing everything vital—she'll try to cut it out, burn it out, beat it out, anything that will give her a chance to win against it. She'll fight with every ounce within her—and then keep on just as a butchered chicken continues to run. She knows someday the blood will run out and she'll have to stop dead—only that tiny spark of hope inside her hopes she'll win living, instead of dying.

Then she hears you, or maybe someone else on the outside say; "get away, you're too much hassle; stop acting and grow up; she's just pretending; she's just a liar; she's no good". . . . And you wonder why she feels beaten down so far that she walks away and quits.

Day to day living and working becomes a masterpiece in creativity that drains every ounce of energy as she tries to protect herself from more hurt.

I don't pretend to think that this explains all multiples, or even the entire experience of any single multiple. This is simply what I have been able to put into words, based on my own experience. My hope is this: just as understanding one complicated mathematical function enables you to comprehend others, maybe understanding one person's experience will enable you to understand, embrace, help, and aid in the healing of another person with MPD.

Before I Die

Gayle R.

It is late autumn
    and the leaves are gently
    blowing in the breeze as
    if they are being caressed
    and kissed.

But, alas, they will die
    and fall to the ground
    even though they know
    not why.

I sometimes wonder will
    I ever be kissed or caressed
    before I die?

Thoughts of an Invisible Survivor

By Jim W.

Speaking as a victim of Multiple Personality Disorder, a professional journalist with a graduate-level education, and the editor and publisher of a peer support and discussion publication of my own, I was moved to address the call for submissions by a letter in a "Dear Abby" column on the "anomalous" case of a "battered man."

The letter once again reminded me of a curious fact that seems to hold true for practically everything I've ever seen written (or broadcast) about MPD, physical and sexual abuse, and the survivors of incest—the victims and survivors are almost always assumed to be female. Indeed, male survivors are ignored: peer support groups are billed "for women"; the few publications I've seen on the issue are edited and written by women for an exclusively female audience; even therapists (who ought to know better) often refuse to accept male survivors as clients due to the necessity of so-called "re-parenting" or regressive work, because of a seldom-stated but fear-tinged worry about sexual elements creeping into the relationship. And when male multiples *are* considered, there seems to be an automatic assumption that they are all sleazy brain-damaged dope fiends or serial killers (e.g., media accounts of male multiplicity invariably cite the case of William "Billy" Milligan). This has very often irritated me. I am not a criminal, an addict, or morally sterile; I've never even gotten a traffic ticket.

The very statistics on MPD, abuse and incest, the way in which these are reported, and the nature of the self-help books, groups, and so forth all tend to be stereotyped and stigmatizing for male survivors—and the falsified myths thus generated (and reinforced by sensationalized television shows) grow ever more difficult to combat since they are becoming so prevalent. You know these myths: all abusers are men; the fathers of young daughters are either drooling perverts or cold-sweat potential rapists just barely held in check; men are abusers but never victims. While it is true that girls are frequently victims of their fathers, uncles, brothers, etc., no one seems to consider the fact that boys can be and are violated by their mothers, sisters, aunts, and so on. (If so few males are victims, how do we explain the oft-cited statistics reporting that some 90% of child molesters and 50% of rapists are survivors of child abuse?) Incest of male children may seldom be acknowledged, but I can personally assure the reader that mothers can and do assault and abuse sons—and, at least in my case, the result has been my own MPD condition.

From a social standpoint, perhaps the saddest part of this issue is that society's traditional demands on the male to "be strong" can humiliate him into keeping silent, though there are few, if any, significant differences in recovery issues faced by men and women. Whatever fears we may have of each other were implanted in us by our abusers, both male and female—but surely in 4,000 years we have gotten beyond the Old Testament pronouncement of "visiting the iniquity of the fathers upon the children, unto the third and fourth generation."

2

PAIN

*My mind kept wondering what awful things
happened to me as a child to have caused this? I
was and still am afraid to know all the details.*
—*Vickie G.*

*If people would stop, look, and listen, then they
could see that we are because of the real world—
we reflect how it really is out there.*
—*Jo Anne M.*

PAIN! That is what I wish I knew about, my therapist knew about, and my
friends and family knew about when I was diagnosed with MPD. And yet,
I do not think that there is any way any of us could have been prepared for
the horror involved in dealing with this disorder.

In a way, I am thankful that I didn't know what would be involved in
dealing with MPD. Because if I had known ahead of time, I might not
have had the strength to venture down the path to recovery.

Death has seemed a viable and comforting alternative at many times
to the tragedy my therapist and I have dealt with.

I don't think either of us were prepared for the excruciating experiences that led to the development of my many alters. As each personality's
story unfolds, pain and suffering become more evident and more unbearable.

I have experienced a lot of physical pain in my life due to a birth
defect, and I have had over forty surgeries in my lifetime (so far), but
none of the pain or humiliation involved with that disorder could hold a
candle to the pain I have suffered emotionally in dealing with MPD.

I have known what it means to feel "different" from others because
of the way I look and I have been ridiculed about my appearance, but

47

again, nothing can compare to how "different" MPD makes me feel from other "normal" people. —Jan C.

Just to be told that the tests show that you were abused as a child is overwhelming. It was not until later that MPD was presented. The idea of abuse alone is incomprehensible to me, for I believed that I came from a better-than-most white American family. My father had money.

I can honestly say that if I truly knew about and understood MPD and where it came from, I never would have chosen to go on. But then, how did I get to the counselor's at first? It was overwhelming depression, suicide, etc., that was driving me. Had I known what was in store for me, what was wrong, and what I needed to do to be healed, I never would have chosen to do it. Death would have been easier and much less painful.

I also wish that there was more factual information on MPD, both for the patient and the family, so that behaviors and actions were more understandable. —Louise H.

To Care

Gayle R.

What is to care?
A four letter word—
    the same as to beat

which is what my
mother did for
she did not care

Now I cannot care
unless I heal
which is also
a four letter word—

When will I care?

I'm writing from the hospital. One thing I truly wished I had known about was the tremendous amount of pain associated with the reliving of memories; that which the holders of grief and the holders of anger manage to force on the body. Someday I hope to understand why this is necessary. I've been in pain associated with this condition since thirteen (now fifty-six) but the last five years have been outrageous. This is my eighth hospitalization for Tri-Geminal Neuritis. I cannot help but wonder about those who do not have good medical coverage. —Isobel M.

No Safe Place

By Serena

When I was diagnosed with MPD, I was not told how long it would take to become functionally integrated and how much debt it would cause me to sustain the rest of my life.

No one told me (a ritual abuse survivor) that my chances of being recontacted, harassed, and reabused were very high.

I was not informed that MPD would cause me to "lose time" long enough to be put into a dangerous position of vulnerability to the occult.

Therapy was not a choice, but the only means to continue living with the stark reality of my abuse.

The possibility that my child would be abused by inner personalities and/or other unaware occult participants suffering from MPD was not explained to me or my husband. My family was left to bear the damage and destruction of reabuse and financial burdens with no caution or guidance.

I wish I had known that my MPD would cause destruction in my marriage that still haunts and strains the intact-yet-failing relationship.

I wish I had been forewarned to beware of other MPD ritual abuse sufferers, so to not expose myself and daughter to being victims.

My lack of a support system caused me to reach out to anyone who could understand with me this terrible realization of my hidden truths.

I wish I had known that my therapist would go from loving/accepting and friendly to being aloof, resentful of debt, and scrupulous with boundaries.

When I was diagnosed, I was asked about the word "safety." I wish

I had been told that there would be no such "safety" for us until all people within had disclosed.

Even though I was told it would take several years, I thought if I worked hard and stayed motivated I could do it in less time. Those are basic requirements and it's still taking years. I wish I had known that treatment would keep me from working (although the MPD also kept me from working).

I wish I had known ahead of time the many ways insurance companies could leave me with high hospital bills because they could use the escape clause of "not medically necessary" to say hospitalization was not warranted. Treatment has wiped out my savings, put me heavily in debt, and if it wasn't for the generosity and flexibility of my therapist, I could no longer afford competent treatment. —Alice O.

I wish I could be guaranteed good results on a weekly or monthly basis, and that progress would be evident from my therapy sessions. I get very discouraged with what I feel is a lack of progress. Perhaps, it is *not* worth the *time*, *effort*, *money* and *pain*; maybe I'd be better off undiagnosed.

When I first got the diagnosis, I felt unintimidated by it. MPD made sense of a lot of things that had happened and of the way I felt. Now, almost two years later, I am intimidated by the diagnosis, burned out by therapy. —Patricia M.

Varnish

by Gregory B.

Another fall day, grey skies with mist and rain. It was the kind of day that calls you to warm dens and warmer steamy ironing. It also calls you to think and to reflect upon the ending season, to write them and remember the good things. To stop and enjoy the warmth of the heat on your face and the moments at your back. It calls you to keep and capture those things that mean so much, that are so often taken for granted.

A day like today also calls me to boxes of dulled crayons that need sharpening and blunting brushes. Brushes that need replacing but seem so friendly, so familiar it makes the thought of replacing them sad.

A student in my art class used to tell me that if you sucked on them, and then kind of puckered them into shape as you pulled them from your mouth, they would stay crisp longer. But this never worked for me. They somehow always ended up as fans on the end of a stick, waiting for nothing except an occasional white cloud or yellow wheat field. So eventually, on days like today, I store them away. Or even worse, I banish them to the varnish drawer. There they lie in the dark until something needs varnishing. Maybe a frame, or a silk screen canvas that has become worn down. A chipped bed rung or the corner of a dropped plaque. Then they dab and fix. They dare a little, dare to feel what it's like to paint again. To be filled with something and let it go.

Once the project is over they are left dangling over the corner of some box or table to dry. Varnish is a sticky thing and cleaning it from a brush is just too messy of a thing, instead you let them dry and throw them to the cats. You let them harden and varnish themselves into a sad little memorial of what they once were. What once filled them now keeps them silent. Preserved for eternity, except to be knocked about the halls by fickle paws.

So today I replaced my brushes, stared out the windows with crayons sharp and brushes crisp, ready to catch the season, to put it on paper. I sit ready to ponder secrets, listening to the cats bat brushes down a long echoing hall.

✺

I wish I knew how complicated therapy was going to be. I wish I knew that it was going to totally encompass my entire life, seeming to leave anything that smacks of normalcy in the hands of the rest of the world.

As the multiplicity and all its characters and characteristics became more pronounced, friends just drifted away. How many times can you tell a person, "Gee, I'm sorry I missed our getting together Friday night, but I unexpectedly ended up in Arizona."

People can only tolerate so much. It has now reached a point where any meaningful or lasting personal relationship is virtually impossible.

That makes the whole thing even more difficult, because we need other people too and not just those within our system. —Virginia C.

I wish I could convey accurately to others the feelings of complete help-lessness and hopelessness that so often overwhelm me. These usually manifest themselves in panic attacks and are occasionally accompanied by suicidal feelings.

I've been in therapy for some time and have made much progress, but these feelings remain. The inner turmoil is often so intense that functioning as a human being is difficult, sometimes impossible.

What I need most from therapists, family, and friends is encouragement, the reassurance to keep on going. I so often want to quit and just give up. It seems too hard, too long, an impossible road to travel. And I wonder, too, if it will be worth it. —Kathleen P.

It's painful and exhausting work, our recovery, and many of us have fought hard against cooperating. —Kathy A.

The aspect of MPD that all counselors, friends and support people should understand is the extreme pain it creates. Pain that is incomprehensible. Not only the physical pain, but the extreme mental anguish of knowing that your family enjoys hurting you, that they do not feel any remorse, and do not care if it kills you or maims you for life. The fact that your pain brings them pleasure is crippling. —Louise H.

I wish I'd known the difficulty of dealing with the tremendous emotional pain that must be experienced and worked through in order to heal. The lack of an understanding support system makes matters worse.

I didn't realize that I would be abandoned by so many people because of who "we" are.

I didn't know that the therapy would go on for so long and that so much more would arise, or that progress would be slow and exhausting.

I wish I'd known that it would be so difficult to unscramble our complex system and that there could be so many fragments that need to be "discovered" to complete the person that I am. —Jo Anne M.

Pain Before Healing

By Sharon S.

The part of my life that has been hurt most is my personal and social life. Once I had a full social life. I was a member of a sports car club for ten years—three of those as secretary. I had friends who were in a band, and I would travel with them to their "gigs." I had friends I would visit and party with.

All of this has come to an end.

I couldn't keep a boyfriend because on the first date, I would switch and one of the other personalities would come out and seduce my date. Of course, my date would think I was "easy"—and there would be no more dates.

I had to stay away from the sports car club, the band and my friends because the other personalities would seduce the girls' husbands or boyfriends. Soon, people began to avoid me. And I was ashamed of the situations I would end up in.

My personal life is in ruins now. I work—at a car dealership and in the composing room of a newspaper—and go home. I can't go out at night for fear of ending up with a stranger in my bed. Sometimes I'll go out for a couple of beers, but I don't stay long.

The hurt, pain, depression, and loneliness is almost unbearable at times and it just gets worse. I feel like an old maid with a lot of life left in me that is just withering away a day at a time.

I fear I will live the rest of my life alone and unwanted because of a disorder that is very strange and hard for others to understand.

CURABLE but sometimes INTOLERABLE by me. I'm told it's curable, that's good, but most of the time I don't believe it. In the midst of the chaos, desolation and depression it's hard to take solace in the idea of a hopeful future. To date, the road to that cure has been long, painful, isolating and full of unexpected, treacherous curves with no end in sight. I guess it's like going for a walk in the woods with a destination in mind. As you truck along and your destination lies ahead, you top the crest of the hill—only to find an endless, murky marsh between you and it. So full of unknown creatures of the dark. Destination reachable? Probably. But is it worth it?

I guess we're human beings deserving of treatment, but usually, we forget that. Please, don't you. Will you hang onto me when I can't?
—Anonymous

Up Against the Walls

by Beverly R.

I have been incorrectly diagnosed as having depression (occasional and severe), psychosis, neurosis . . . and the list goes on. I don't think Schizophrenia was ever used. Manic depressive was probably the most popular. All of the incorrect diagnoses are actually symptoms of MPD and characteristics of my many people.

Through all of my mental illness trials and tribulations I never felt crazy or out of control. Now that I have been diagnosed as a multiple I feel like a freak. I am having a hard time believing that I can have a healthy relationship with anyone, especially a man. I am feeling very lonely and empty. Now that I know what is wrong with me I am terrified that my people will come out inappropriately. I do not have control over them right now. My therapist says as I become more integrated I will have control and everyone will work as one.

For years no one could pinpoint what was wrong with me. I was tested and examined from head to toe many times. Even though everyone—doctors, family and friends—tried to help me, I was beyond help. Nothing worked.

Finally, in desperation I agreed to have shock treatments. I had fourteen. Ignorant people believe shock treatments diminish brain activity and make a person dull and lifeless, rather like having a lobotomy. The movies and television have painted the procedure as a painful one, always done as punishment, and against the patient's will.

This is not so. I received excellent care before and after each treatment. There was no brutality involved and I can honestly say my mind is as quick as ever.

Unfortunately, even with the shock treatments, I continued to try to commit suicide. There seemed to be no hope. I had quit my job, lost my apartment, my plants died, and my family paid my bills.

But you know what? I didn't care. At all. Not even a little. I just flat *didn't care* if I lived or died.

The strongest memory I have about that whole time is that there was no anger, sadness or even guilt. In fact, there were no feelings at all. Every time I hurt myself, it was always very quiet and methodical. There was never any hysteria or confusion. I just felt that it was the right thing to do.

I now know it was one of my inside people hurting me.

I do not blame anyone for anything. I am not ashamed, nor do I feel guilty about anything I did or said. Nor do I feel shame about the hospitals I have been in. If I had not been committed I would never have met the therapist who is helping me now and I would probably be dead.

Things in my life aren't working and I know it. I do not have a social life. I am a workaholic. My life is empty and I have no friends.

I have finally accepted that I am a multiple. I can no longer deny who and what I am. It makes sense out of a life that has never made sense to me or anyone else for that matter.

My purpose in this life is clear. I have given considerable thought to whether or not I should leave this life for the next. It all seems so overwhelming and I really wonder if I have the strength to see it through to fruition.

The obstacles are many. Reactions from family, friends and coworkers are what I fear the most. I know I will be rejected and ridiculed by some. I don't know if I am strong enough to deal with that.

This isn't like substance abuse where there is something tangible to avoid, or a physical deformity that is easy to detect. This is inside, the essence of my being. If I make it go away I go away. If I deny that my people exist then I don't exist.

Retreat . . .

back
into
my
mind.
Never
come
out.
Hurt
too
much.
All
outside
tears

beyond
words.
Do
you
care?
—Ann H.

Running

By Gregory B.

Even though the actions are long dead their dreams slapped me in the face as I slept.

The silent scream and the rush of air filling my chest tell me I am awake. I have to be. Looking around the room I find my wife gently sleeping and the moon slipping in through the fold in the blinds. The light falls on the cat cutting her into sleeping ribbons. I feel my heart slow and the beating in my ears quiet. My fingers tingle as the heater kicks on, then off. I sit twisted among sheets and blankets trying to pull the visions from my mind. I sit in a dark room sifting fear from reality, like a boy in a sand pile. I am left with visions from my mind. I am left with one large mountain, finding both fear and reality are the same.

I go to run in the park across the street from my home. It's a green little mirage full of promise and dew. It is full of twisting trails and creaky wooden bridges. I can remember the fall leaves gathering into piles under the bridges and children jumping off to land in them rolling and yelping and then climbing in them again to do the same.

I know every meter of this old trail, every tree, every fox crossing. I know it leads to another park and then a biking trail and then the university. I have run it a thousand times. I have stood in its aerobic area doing pull-ups in the dark, until I am exhausted and drop to the ground and land in the sand. But today, amidst the sun and shadows, I can't catch my breath. My mind spins and I feel someone following me. I feel his eyes on my shoulder and his feet just missing my heels. It is in the middle of the day in Fort Worth and my heart is ripping through my chest. It is being pulled toward the sun and I stand hanging in the wind on a running path.

Silence. Watching and ready. Turning, and again to see the man I feel just inches behind me. Deep breath. He's gone, or was it just a child on a skateboard? Or, was he there? My eyes begin to well up with tears, the fear passes and I decide to walk behind some old couple out walking their dog. I relax a little. Then I know I am going crazy.

I try to flick my thumb against my palm clicking my ring. My ring is gone. No it's on the other hand. And which hand has my watch? Damn, wrong one. Even looking at my hands it feels as if my ring is on the wrong hand.

I can hardly drive anywhere in Dallas any more, I always take the wrong exit. East? West? I don't know. North? South? What do they mean? I do not know right and left, I think.

I bought a compass. It helps.

Where is my mind? My thoughts? They race each other until I can only see the places they have been. All blurred like a cartoon car taking off in a chase. I can't slow them, I can't even see them anymore. I just stand back and look where they usually are projected.

Then it stopped. A lady reached out her hand to touch mine. She told me there are lots of men like me. She said that in time the terror would end. She said the pain wasn't my fault, or the abuse either. I believed her. Months later I knew I wasn't losing my mind, insanity wasn't tearing at my face. I had nothing to lose in this madness. It was something coming out, not going in.

Crazy isn't some place to go, for me it was where I had been.

The Breaking Point

By Susan W.

It was coming. If she had been a small animal she would have stood up on her hind legs and sniffed the air. She could smell it, feel it. The hair on the back of her arms stood up all by itself. The fact that she was so young did not matter. She had quickly developed the innate ability to sense danger. Unfortunately, there was nothing she could do about it.

She heard the sound of glass breaking and knew that her mother had finished the bottle she'd been drinking. Now it was time to wait. Minutes . . . hours . . . she sat on the edge of the bed in her bedroom without a door, waiting for the first creak of the steps which meant Momma was coming.

Momma was coming! Momma was coming! Sometimes it sounded to her like the rhythm of the trains on the railroad tracks across the street. Momma was coming! Momma was coming! A real, live bogeyman, stinking of gin and sweat and she was coming up the steps to beat her senseless. Momma was going to beat her until Momma couldn't raise her arms anymore. Momma was going to kick her until she couldn't get up off the floor. Maybe Momma would get extra careless and knock her down the steps again. Maybe not. Maybe Momma would just forget to feed her for two or three days. Maybe Momma would forget that she was only six years old and couldn't figure out how to get food for herself.

She sat, waiting. Actually, the waiting didn't bother her very much. It wasn't as if she might not get beaten. She knew that she would. It wasn't the waiting that bothered her. It was the knowing. She knew as surely as she knew the scabs and scars on her body that Momma was coming up those steps and she wasn't coming to hug her. Sometimes the sun would set before Momma would come up the steps and the stairway would be very dark—too dark to see. But she could hear the steps creaking anyway as she strained her eyes to see. She would sit in the dark listening to the stairs creak and her heart beat and she would try to decide which was louder. In the end, it didn't really matter because the sounds of the beating drowned out everything else.

She had long since stopped crying out. In fact she was remarkably well behaved. As Momma lumbered up the steps the little girl would begin to take off her clothes. She would fold them in a neat pile and lay them at the foot of the bed, out of the way of the beating area. Momma always said that she wouldn't beat the clothes she had bought the little girl; truthfully it made sense to the child. Clothes were precious and she could understand not wanting to damage them.

The beating. The beating could go on and on. It depended on Momma's energy. But it really didn't matter how long it continued because the little girl would simply leave her body behind and go out on the swings to play. She would swing high in the sky keeping her eyes on the sun or the moon, going higher and higher until it seemed that she was a part of the sky itself—flying away over the treetops to a place where little girls were loved.

She couldn't exactly explain how it was that she knew when to return but she always did. She would find herself lying on the floor, unable to get up and the room would be dark. Momma would be gone. Sometimes it would take her hours to get up off the floor. Sometimes there would be blood. Sometimes she would just sleep right there because it was easier than crawling into bed. Besides, crawling into bed meant it would be easier for Momma to find her if Momma decided to come back and start all over again, which she had done several times recently.

The little girl lived this life for many, many years. Sometimes she went to school. Sometimes she couldn't because she was too sick. No one ever wondered about the little girl who wore leotards in the heat of the summer. No one ever asked why she was rarely outside playing. In 1958, almost everyone beat their children to one degree or another. Some just went further than others.

Rest in Peace

Billie A.

Where are the words to describe
The devastation of being
Half dead and half alive.
I feel the pain, I know I live
I feel the cold, I know I'm dead
Emotions buried, memories buried.
For such a long, long time.
Tears run down my face.
The anger, the knowing, *so* unkind.
Dig, dig up the things that are so foul.
They come to life! They live! (the memories)
As I tell another person, out loud.
The fears, the hurting, what they did.
What I saw and was forced to do!
Don't feel, don't believe
I grieve and grieve
So the pain will cease.
They (the memories) can truly
Be buried . . . and I can
Rest in *trusting* peace.

How the Person Spent Our Shrink's Week's Vacation

By Many in One Among Ones Among Many

"Good," Cliff said. "She should go away more often. Any therapy is too much therapy, and too much therapy is keeping us broke. Who wants to live on peanut butter sandwiches for the rest of our lives, anyway? Too many sandwiches will turn our somatic reality into a damn girl."

"It's true," Alexis said, "Except that we are a girl. And the reason we can't take a vacation is because she has all our money to take on hers."

"The reason we haven't taken a vacation to date," Rich said, "Is that no one can agree on where to go and what to do when we get there."

"A vacation from too much therapy is vacation enough for me," Cliff said. "Besides, who needs her anyway? We have survived milieus more caustic than a week's absence from her presence. And to live without her will make us a man."

"I hate her," Dillon said. "And I hate her office. She has only stupid chairs, and nothing to play with. I want to go to a child psychiatrist so at least I have something to do when we're there."

"Then maybe her vacation is a good thing," Rich said. "Since at last you are saying something everyone can hear."

"I don't think she likes children anyway," Dillon said. "She doesn't have any of her own."

"She has at least one, but it's inside," Rich said, "Like you."

Shreve said, "I'm going to make one infinitesimal scratch on my leg with a razor blade where she can't see it to mark every day she's gone."

"You can't," Buzz said, "It's specifically against the contract."

"She can't enforce it if we're dead," Shreve said.

"Leave me out of your diabolical machinations," Cliff said. "This is our chance to prove we never needed her anyway. That we can communicate and cooperate without benefit of her therapeutic interventions. Then I can take over where she left off, which is nowhere."

"Then we can leave her since she left us, and her income will suffer," d'Bradt said. "Besides, she will never find anyone as interesting as us to talk to. That will teach her to go away."

"Every time she goes away I think she's going to fall out of an airplane," Dillon said. "I hate her for going away, and I would especially hate her if she fell out of an airplane."

"She has to go away sometimes," Shreve said. "Otherwise she will get burnt out and maybe start yelling at us or something."

Renee said, "This is our opportunity to do all the things we've always wanted to do but didn't, because she would call it acting out. Like, I am going to ask my future boyfriend over for a little fun."

"No one wants your boyfriend," Cliff said. "It would be just like you to get what you're after and then disappear. I'd have to take over and punch him out."

"Why can't you go away for once and leave me alone?" Renee said. "I haven't had any fun since we started therapy. We used to have good times, like when I got you that radical lesbian who thought she was dating Patt."

"That was hilarious," d'Bradt said. "One advantage to multiplicity is you can see someone but they can't see you."

Buzz said, "There will be no boyfriend or girlfriend or any friend. And if any person tries to touch me in any way I will fucking kill them. Maybe you want to hear about how?"

"You and Cliff belong in reform school," Alexis said. "Then maybe I could visit my father and mother who love me. This would be the perfect time, since the shrink indicates that it is contraindicated. She would never have to know about it."

"You think," Patt said, "that in their senescence they are in North Carolina eager for our presence in a way they never were in our past. But who do you think *they* think we are? They refuse to call even the legal entity by her elected name. The reality is that they are living inside us as we speak, engineering a psychogenic death on the installment plan. And they are stronger than the shrink, and they will win."

"The way out of the things that make us want to run and to find our way back into ourselves is barred by two doorkeepers," Rich said, "Ivan-the-Terrible and Katherine-the-Great. They torture us with phantom reminiscences and evanescent vestiges of the past that live on in the present and presage the future."

"They live in the black hole inside our soul," Buzz said. "Maybe the shrink will help us kill them."

"That, too, is against the contract," Rich said.

"Then how are we going to spend the shrink's vacation?" d'Bradt said. "No one gets to do any damn thing they want to do. Everything Buzz wants to do is illegal, everything Shreve wants to do is an infraction of the contract, and Alexis would get us a one-way ticket to North Carolina and the insane asylum. Renee is going to get us pregnant, Dillon is

61

going to decompensate in the corner and cost us our job, Rich tries to make us go to twelve-step meetings, but Cliff won't let us out of the apartment. Patt wants nothing. Myself, I would like to sneak away on our own vacation and let her wonder where we are when she returns."

"I think the time has come to write The Great American Novel," Rich said. "Because the shrink has seen us, we have seen ourselves, and now the world is going to see Ivan-the-Terrible and Katherine-the-Great who have made us many running apart. Then our progenitors will be more dysphoric inside us than outside us when they see we can take outside the inside we took inside from the outside, and the world will see who they are in a way they never saw us. Then it will be their turn to run and hide.

Maybe we all had a different childhood, but that it was lousy, and that they took place severally in one somatic reality which never forgets even when we do. That is one thing we can all agree on. Through The Great American Novel, we will make ourselves out of many, one."

"In the words of André Malraux," Cliff said, "On the road to vengeance one finds life."

I wish I had been advised to tell my regular physician what types of physical symptoms might occur as a result of MPD. He gave me a narcotic for migraine headaches which, following an unintentional overdose, caused me to dissociate on an almost continuous basis, gave me the appearance of psychotic behavior, and backed up in my kidneys.
—Anne M.

For My Sisters

Kimberly J.

They bubble up
like hot springs
these long forgotten memories.

Knowing but not wanting to know
the deep, dark secrets
from another time, another place.

Taking the form of a vision:
a man and a child
seen from the outside, looking in as if it were not me
knowing all the while it is.

The shape of a sphere
red, hot and pounding
inside my head.

Recognizing the pain,
the heat, the color,
yet no words for the memory.

Knowledge, but too young to have the words
or the meaning,
yet old enough to know.

The pain shuts off the words
unable to feel it
and say it at the same time.

Words choking at my throat
I gasp for breath
while the pain glows a little brighter.

The pain
revulsion and shame
keep the words from tumbling out.

If never spoken perhaps never true.

Night Thoughts

By Gregory B.

When I was small I would lie in the bed my mother and father bought at a garage sale. It was warm and I would quietly listen to the sounds of muffled voices from my parents room. I could never understand what they were saying, but would recognize the inflection of a question or the quick pace of a laugh. I could hear them answer the phone or get out of bed, and I would try to figure out what they were saying, why they would laugh. I would imagine they were discussing me. Finally I would fall asleep before the conversations stopped.

But tonight I don't hear recognizable voices, or see familiar shapes in a dark room. I smell chlorine and my throat chokes me as I dream. Tonight, I hear a playground bell ringing. I hear groups of boys laughing. I smell urine burning on old steam heaters in my grade school. I wake to find I am wet with perspiration and my lip is bleeding.

In my father's home I can walk from my bedroom, through the kitchen, into the dining room, front room, and back again never opening my eyes. I know every step and have walked them thousands of times, lights on and lights off. I can hear the whisper of our icebox fan if the door is only slightly ajar. I can hear June bugs hitting the light near the backdoor if I have forgotten to turn it off. And I can figure how long my brother has been driving his jeep by listening to it cool outside my window.

But now I hear cats crying and a boy hitting stones with a stick. They hit the corrugated metal fence and ping. Cans start and stop as they roll empty down the street. Someone screams, I think it's a scream. So much means little to me. I notice the unmistakable absence of dogs barking and music playing. There are no crickets. I see few lights to fill the windows or moving lights from moving cars. Odd birds coo while sitting on my

64

window but even they speak in tongues too garbled to give away any secrets. How do I know they have secrets? Secrets—one upon the other like the stones that make up the walls that keep the cold out.

In this room with queer green tile and cold stone floors, I quietly talk inside myself, remembering miles to the west a man and his wife lie in bed mumbling amidst themselves. They answer the phone, walk about in the house without turning on the lights and hear the sounds of bugs wondering what strange new sounds I hear as I lie falling asleep miles away from home. They could never imagine what I hear, they missed them all the first time.

Someday I will tell them of these nights, of being followed, of always being ready to run. I will tell them the meaning of strange sounds—the message of odd sights. I will share with them my keening—tell them of my secrets.

How should they have know I have secrets? Secrets one upon the other, like the stones that make up the walls that keep the cold out. Secrets? Sexual secrets? Secrets of men on men. Pain-filled secrets. Secrets that roll through my mind, starting and stopping. Secrets that don't have words to describe them. Memories that coo and land on the window waking me in the night to smell chlorine.

How does one know what goes on behind a wall that keeps the cold out? Or inside a room with a bed bought at a garage sale? How does one know what goes on in a green tiled bathroom at school? Or, in a chlorine filled bathhouse next door?

Children, they whisper secrets, quietly at first. But you can hear them, if you're listening. They are the discovery of a boy sitting alone in a dark room listening to the silence. They are the taste of salty tears and iron blood. They are the wide shapes of boy's eyes as he watches terror with familiarity.

They are the color of red and black and blue.

The Skills of our Tribe

Ann H.

Each child is taught
Their tribe's skills.
We were the best-behaved
Children on the block—
Terrified to be otherwise.

Pretending, mistrusting,
Energy only for survival—
No sense of self.

Mother, Father,
For what future
Did you prepare us?
Did you think the earth
Doomed?
Or was only our tribe
Planned for extinction?

You Have Filled Up the Whole World

Ann H.

Mother, you have filled up
The whole world with
Your anger.
Just as I have.
There is no room
For other people.
Perhaps you can feel others
In the intensity of combat.
But mostly I feel
Very alone.

6 Years Old

Gayle R.

You stood
    and
I crouched

You beat
    and
I fled

Inside where
    the terror was trapped
    as I watched you take

My little girl's body
    and squeeze and shake and beat it
    to your heart's desire

While I stood far inside
    and screamed to the corners
    of my soul

To stop this madness.
    But you are my mother
      And things did not change.

You Were All I Knew

Susan P.

You didn't know when to stop.
So you made me like you.

By turning the care
and the comfort
into force
and tying and twisting it all
into cruelty and crimes
on a child
small
without ways to fight back,
you cut me deeper
than any knife
could ever dream.

When you cut your wrists
and bled tears
of pain and blood,
you also cut me
inside.
You cut me into parts.
And while you bled,
I bled too.
I bled where you could not see.
I bled within.
I bled without blood,
but not without pain.
And I bled again and again
as your force
and hands
invaded me
and cut the parts into parts into parts
until there was no me,
only you
and my method

of living
with you.
And while I hid, I could not escape.
You were all I knew.
And there you were
dying each day
as I watched.
And you were my Mom.

To My Sister and Brother

By Kathy O.

I've given you only sketchy details about what Dad did to me, and even less information about the nightmare I lived under our beloved mother. What good would the telling do? You have your memories of childhood, I have mine.

My fondest wish is for you to hear what I do say. Don't minimize what I've been through or what I face. You may not believe in the *we* that is my life. For you and for me we generally present the *I*. You may not understand. If you want to, ask me to explain or offer suggestions about what to read.

If there are no "monsters" in your childhoods, I'm happy for you both. There were in mine. I don't need "sugar pills" like "keep busy" or "just go to work and forget about all of it." I have a long and difficult road ahead. I'm shattered. The *I* became *we* and all of us have a lot to deal with and it will be slow and painful.

We'd like your support but if you insist on wanting to wish it all away, we may all draw back. Silence and pretending were staples in a shattered world. To be healthy, we need to be open and to face what was and what we have become as a result.

We need to heal, in our own way and at our own speed. Try not to rush us because it would be more comfortable for you.

We all know you act out of love. Yet the nightmare we relive happened in *our* family—not to someone in a book or on TV. We will respect your needs for minimal information about what actually happened.

Please respect us, we are *all* your sisters and brothers.

69

Upon receiving a correct diagnosis, I finally understood why I hated my father for child abuse. Upon emergence of various personalities, I also understood my hatred for my "perfect" mother, who had subjected me to ritual abuse. —Anne M.

For David, Steven and Ellen,
I write this for you, to let people know you were alive. No one knew your pain and suffering but we did. We were there and we saw what they did to you at the rituals. I wish we could have stopped them but we were too afraid. After you died you were no more, just like you were never born. But you did live and you did die. There was no one to tell you goodbye or let the world know that for a short time you were here and now you're gone.
    But I know and I'll tell them.

Love,
Michael P.

All my life I've been pretty lonely. No one to play with or really talk to. Always afraid to let people know who I was because they might hurt me or have me taken away. I came out a long time ago to protect her when she was little and they took her to rituals. I always wonder if she dies will anyone even know I was here. Will anybody ever know about any of us. No grave to say I was born or when I died. We fight real hard to keep her alive and not know all the bad things that happen to her and take her pain and love her when nobody else did and even she didn't know what we were doing for her and now that our therapist told her, she's afraid and doesn't want to believe we are here, but we are here. We live, we breathe and feel and think and yet no one knows we even exist. If we do come out to other people, we have to pretend we're her and if we mess up, it causes all kinds of trouble and she doesn't know what happened and we feel bad about that but sometimes we just want to be ourselves. I've seen a lot of bad things, and couldn't tell anyone about them. I wish someday I could live like other people and have friends my age, I could go to baseball games and play like other kids but it will never be that way, it can't be, we'll always be alone. We do have one person who cares about us and loves us, our therapist, and that's more than we ever had before. We never had anyone who loves us just for us. We're not bad, we just do what we have to protect her and when we got hurt there was no one there for us to hold us and make us feel better like other kids I see with their mom and dads

70

who hold them when they cry or just hold them because they want to. Sometimes I just want to yell real loud, "I am alive, I do exist."

Michael P. —13 years old

(my therapist says I'm an alter)

Shelters from the Storm

By Jana D.

To: All those who look into our eyes.

Where do I begin? I have many to choose from. Many more than I can remember.

Of those I do remember, where should I start?

I could start with age four when I was sexually abused by a "well loved" neighbor.

I could start at age nine when my teacher stripped me naked, bound my hands and feet, then threw me into a cold shower. All done to punish me for "making up stories about a fine man."

How about age fourteen when someone I loved and who supposedly loved me, beat me with a belt until I screamed and cowered into a corner? If those events aren't traumatic enough, then maybe I should choose the age of fifteen when I was blackmailed into becoming a "brood bitch" for a black-market adoption ring. Maybe I should start with all of the babies born to me that were taken from me either through "adoption" or death.

Where then, does one start? Or more correctly. Where do "many" start?

Maybe the gruesome details of all the traumatic incidents are not the important point. Maybe it is more important to tell you that when you look into our eyes you will see pain; more than many, less than even more. We think (most of us anyway) that the *results* of this pain are the most important consideration.

The results of this pain are "us." Many of us compacted into one body. It is called Multiple Personality Disorder. We would like to explain what this means to us.

MPD means missed days and weeks and for some of us even missed years; missed appointments, birthdays, holidays, weeks and weeks of missed school and work.

It means embarrassment, sadness, humiliation, fear and, most of all, a lifetime of confusion.

Once in awhile, it can even mean some good times. But most importantly, it means survival.

Many would think that the pain of the multiple abuses would be enough to send most into insanity. So why, many may ask, should they also suffer from the multitudes of minds? Suffer? We think not. We do not *suffer from* MPD. We *survive because* of MPD. Without it I and We would have died long ago. MPD is our shelter from the storms.

We have come to the point where many of us have joined or integrated into others and before the end of this life, more will blend to make fewer. We doubt seriously, however, that we will ever fuse to make "one."

We don't consider this such a bad future.

Many people think that multiples must be "one" before they are considered cured. This may be the case for many multiples, and we consider them fortunate. But other multiples, like us, will be grateful for a compromise among our selves. We want people to understand that we may never be considered an individual. We want people's love and respect anyway.

We would like to leave all of you who read this with one thought:

We *all* want and need your love and understanding, so please don't condemn us for being us. Instead, as you look into our eyes, see *our* pain and understand that *all* of us (you and us alike) are, or can become, shelters from the storm.

My Name Is . . .

By Pat M.

"My name is Bill W., I am an alcoholic."

Just so do many alcoholics begin their painful and arduous journey toward the eventual restoration of their health and wellness.

I am not an alcoholic, but I have before me an at least equally enormous journey, and it must begin in much the same way:

"My name is Patricia M., I have MPD."

Such small words to encompass such an immense identity, the reality of which, now two years past diagnosis, I am still struggling to take in as my own. Even given the open question of a history of more abuse as yet undiscovered, I wrestle: do I really have the right (or the courage) to claim MPD for myself? It is awesomely frightening. It is an acknowledgement which for me is also deeply filled with a sense of alienation, failure and shame, because I feel I do not really fit well into the clinical definition of MPD, having (again—as yet?) no knowledge of truly brutal physical or any sexual abuse in my past. As an adjunct to my therapy, I—and sometimes one or more of my alters—read some of the scientific literature on MPD. We have found this to be beneficial in providing a theoretical framework within which to operate, yet for me this comes with a high price to pay in added pain. Against the assaultive ferocity of abuse most frequently written about, my story as we know it thus far is simply "not that awful," so why, then, do I have this mental illness, unless there is some inherent flaw or weakness in my psychological makeup? Even having a clear cognitive understanding of the phenomenon of "minimizing" does not take away the hurt inside that question. This article is thus an attempt to externalize some of the conflicts and deep pain I experience simply in trying to accept my diagnostic label.

I first entered therapy in January 1984, as half of a marriage rapidly and agonizingly failing. Despite some gaps, I have been working with the same therapist ever since. Very early on he started: "You were abused," he would flatly, though gently, say to me. And I, just as flatly—and probably less gently—would tell him no, it had not been so. I still had my control in those days, but little did I suspect how fragile that control was becoming, or how awfully it would be tried. I did not cry then, no matter how devastating those early marital counseling sessions were. I could sum up my entire life in a very few, *very* carefully neutral and spare words:

I WAS ALWAYS DIFFERENT, I NEVER FIT IN; I WAS NOT EVER A LOVED OR WANTED CHILD; MY PARENTS WERE NOT PHYSICALLY DEMONSTRATIVE PEOPLE; WE WERE TOO MANY (TWO ADULTS AND SIX CHILDREN) CROWDED INTO TOO LITTLE SPACE (ONE TWO-BEDROOM FLOOR OF A DUPLEX), BUT NO ONE *EVER* TOUCHED ANYONE ELSE EXCEPT IN A BRUSQUE OR PUNITIVE WAY; NO ONE SPOKE TO ANYONE AT ALL IN THE MORNINGS; I CAN NOT REMEMBER MY MOTHER EVER TOUCHING ME GENTLY AND THE LAST TIME I REMEMBER MY FATHER HOLDING ME I WAS THREE YEARS OLD. I DO NOT REMEMBER MUCH ELSE OF THE TIME BEFORE I WAS FOURTEEN YEARS OLD; AT FOURTEEN, WITH

THE CHANGE TO A NEW SCHOOL, I MADE A CONSCIOUS DECISION THAT THE PAST NO LONGER EXISTED, AND I COULD START ALL OVER AGAIN AND BE WHOEVER I WANTED TO BE; THE NEXT SEVERAL YEARS WERE FULL OF SUICIDAL FEELINGS, THE DESIRE TO RUN AWAY, FEELINGS OF REPEATEDLY EXPLODING WITHIN AND NEEDING TO PUT MY JAGGED PIECES BACK TOGETHER AGAIN, CONTINUAL HEADACHES AND PAIN, PAIN, PAIN; AT EIGHTEEN, MY PARENTS DIVORCED; AT NINETEEN, I MOVED OUT OF MY FATHER'S HOUSE; I EARNED A BACHELOR OF ARTS DEGREE IN CHILD PSYCHOLOGY, GOT MARRIED, HAD TWO CHILDREN, EARNED A BACHELOR OF SCIENCE DEGREE IN ELEMENTARY EDUCATION, FOUND A JOB TEACHING, AND THEN MY MARRIAGE FELL APART. END OF STORY.

Except that my therapist, who heard all I was not saying, did not buy it. "You were abused," he continued to say.

God, how I hated—and feared—him for it! At least once I terminated therapy, unready yet to trust him with my pain.

In the summer of 1986, new pain piled on new pain piled on old, old pain; my precious control started to break down. Overwhelmed by grief I could not express, we began therapy again, and now, as I was losing that so-necessary control, I started losing time, or getting time mixed up, and I can no longer tell my story in sequence.

Each time I saw him, I felt I had, at all costs, to defend against those words, "You were abused."

But bit by bit, he was earning my trust, and I could tell him of smaller hurts, far away from my deepest pain. I could not even yet trust myself to know the secrets of my own story.

The next summer, in 1987, he came back from vacation and as cautiously and gently as he could, he exploded the bomb that wounds me still. In the instant before the pain hit, the Little One inside me knew she had been seen, and I knew our truth and was terrified of it:

MY NAME IS PATRICIA M. I, AND ALL THE OTHER "MY NAME IS" ALTERS WITHIN ME, *WE* HAVE MPD.

And since that time, much (but not, I am afraid, all) hell has broken loose.

I can concede the truth of the flashbacks or abreactions I experience. I understand now the nights when someone inside cries all night, or another one has nightmares, or one is simply awake and watchful while

74

the rest sleep. I can accept not always remembering things. I can identify and acknowledge the names and personalities of the alters we have met. I hear their voices. I see them in the room where we all go for therapy. I hurt for their hurts. I do not doubt that we have MPD. What I cannot seem to accept is that we were, in fact, abused, and the abuse was sufficient to necessitate the creation of different personalities to cope with it all.

Abuse is typically written about in the scientific literature and in the popular press, as horribly awful physical maltreatment or sexual assault, resulting in real, verifiable injuries or the destruction of the body. That did not happen to me.

Yes, there were some specific traumatic events, and some punishments that could be considered abusive, but not excessively so. No, the abuse done to me was, for the most part, "only" emotional, and so I feel alienated from the other "really abused," "real" MPD clients.

I feel shame, because I failed to cope well with what was, after all, "not that bad."

One who is physically or sexually abused can say, "This is how I hurt, where I hurt, and why I hurt. I have the right to feel pain." And everyone can see that this is, indeed, true. I cannot say that. No one can see where I have hurt. I was "only" repeatedly abandoned for hours on end as an infant, screaming with hunger and cold and wet and the terror of being alone. I was "only" incessantly bludgeoned by scorn and ridicule from parents, from siblings, from peers. I was only a failure at everything I tried, a constant source of disappointment to my father. I was "only" never good enough, never loveable enough, a constant source of irritation and anger for my mother. I was "only" continually shunned by, forgotten about, or kept away from the others in my household. I "only" had every person and every thing I was foolish enough to love taken away from me. I was "only" lost in my own family, not heard, not seen, not touched, not acknowledged in any positive way, neither cared about nor cared for.

There was an aunt who lived upstairs from us who did try to do whatever she could when she was home. She moved out of state when I was nine years old, and, fearing for my emotional health in that house, she wanted to take me away with her. But I had no visible bruises, no broken bones or scars from stitches. I was only emotionally battered, and she felt she had no right to take me from my family.

Except . . . except . . . except—what greater pain and damage can be done to a child than to deny the child's very existence? Mira Rothenberg, in her book about the work she did with severely disturbed children, *Children With Emerald Eyes*, (The Dial Press, New York, NY, 1977) describes two-and-one-half-year-old Danny's experience of being physically lost in the woods for two days, in the following way:

> I've often tried to imagine what it must be like to be lost. Lost in unfamiliar woods. Lost when you are two-and-a-half years-old. Lost for two endlessly long days. How many hours are there in a day? How long is eternity? How long is infinity for a two-and-a-half year-old child? As long as a night? What do two nights make? A forever, a death, an abandonment? Yet, I can't. The scope is beyond me. I cannot comprehend the magnitude of the terror, the feeling of abandonment, of impending death, of all the bogeymen when the night comes close and engulfs you. When the hunger makes your stomach ache, when the thirst parches your throat. When does it end? Ever? And the noises, real and imaginary, and the animals and the walking trees. And all the goblins and all the witches and all the all . . . .
>
> The physical discomfort is obvious, but what about the psychic one? No one to take care of you, no one to attend to you—lost. What about the feeling of being lost—losing identity, losing self in the morass of the many feelings which the child must have experienced but could not control. Danny could not find his self among all of them. The security of self got drowned, overwhelmed by all his terrors, and Danny got lost . . . .
>
> What is mental illness if not a getting lost of the self, for whatever reason. Danny experienced it concretely in the forest but then forever he experienced it in all aspects of his life.
>
> "Be lost." It is a feeling both of body and mind. For when one is truly lost, all connections are severed and the vacuum this produces—the terror and insecurity—must be overwhelming. (p.167)

The Baby within me (who still inconsolably screams that terror) understands Danny completely. And Nobody, too, (an older alter, but still a child), knows with exquisite pain the confusion: "Do I really exist? Am I really a real girl?"

And still I struggle to accept that I was abused, and that therefore, I too, can say I have a right to my pain, without feeling ashamed of myself for having failed to cope better. There are no x-rays that will show where I was broken, no visible scars mark where I have bled. Almost, I could wish my body had been battered, because bodies either heal or die. For the injured body in the hands of a skilled caregiver, healing is largely a matter of when, not if. New skin grows, bruises fade, bones knit together again. But what of a child's beaten and savaged spirit? No stitches can repair a child's shredded self-esteem. No plaster can set the shattered sense of self. No machines or hands can find all the bruised and bleeding places, no anesthetic can ever take the edge off the pain. Our hurts are hidden and secret, but no less real than others you can see. Emotional abuse, abandonment and neglect may not be as sensational as physical or sexual abuse, but those of us who have MPD as a result of it may need more support and encouragement to get beyond our shame and claim the right, not only to know and feel our pain, but also to be healed of it.

"My name is Patricia M. I was abused, and I have MPD."

I still am not yet able to own those words "whole-heartedly," though I believe parts of me can. My therapist has fought long and hard beside me to get this far, and we still have a long way to go. Perhaps one day, when we really have accepted the label and all it means, healing will no longer be a matter of *if*. It will become a matter of *when*.

In my family of three brothers and three sisters, one brother committed suicide and two others are alcoholic. All three girls, including myself, were raped by family members. My father used to threaten to kill us in addition to delivering severe beatings and abuse.

Today my parents go to church, live quietly and travel. They have never been sorry, and consider us bad children. Their denial is so strong that it is unreal. They will not admit to these acts. To them, it's as if it never happened. If we even bring it up they tell us what's wrong with us, not them.

It's difficult for outsiders to understand this, so they try to be peacemakers. Sometimes it's better to walk away from the abusive family and live well than to spend your life wishing for and trying to make them different. When we walk away we should not feel guilty. We are trying to survive. —Kathy C.

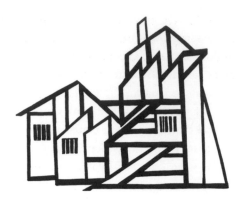

Abuse: A Trauma That Never Ends

By Nancy G.

As I lie on the hard mattress and hear the clank as they close and lock the steel doors to "the tank" of the county jail, we have time, plenty of time, to contemplate how all of us traveling under the umbrella name of "Nancy" could have ended up here in this jail cell, alone, deserted and in deep legal trouble. My deep legal problems came as a result of desperately trying to put an end to the physical, sexual and emotional abuse that had been occurring for generations in my family and was continuing for another generation. [Nancy was jailed for contempt of court after attempting to block her father's visitation/access.]

My mind has time to traverse all the memories we hold of our whole life, but the pain it brings us is too great and we can't seem to get past the first bitter and painful memories. So, we close our eyes, hoping against hope that we'll wake up in that two story house with the white picket fence that we dreamed about as a small child. There, baby blue lilacs grow up the trellis wall and the sweet scent of the lilacs fills our bedroom as we lie safely tucked away in our four poster bed.

The yell of "dinner time" and the clank of the metal trays draws us back to the bitter reality that surrounds us, that has always surrounded us with deep inner sadness. We realize we just traded one set of prison bars for another.

We've always been locked in one prison or another. Our parents built the first one and we, eventually, through the timeless abuse, devised an even larger prison of our own. The only difference is, today we can see the steel prison bars of the jail.

But, our own prison bars are invisible to others. An invisible prison, few can understand, as they spout off how they (unlike us) were able to "put things behind them and stop dwelling on the past tragedies in their lives," or "get on with their lives and quit blaming others, accept responsibility for their own actions."

And once again, we feel different, separate from them and woefully guilty for possessing such glaring character flaws. We reach for our antidote, self-punishment. Once again, we have failed to be "strong, like them." Once again, we failed "to measure up." So the vicious cycle continues and the prison walls never rot away.

We are trapped forever, wanting desperately to be strong like they appear to be. We know that there is something deeply wrong with us and the slightest comment, action, person or even animal can send us off into a world of our own in one of our "out of control states."

Our whole life becomes one of covering up our secrets of dissociation and self abuse. The many voices within direct our life. Our life is never our own and we are not one. We spend hours trying to cover up our "secret lives" and pretend to be so much like "them" as possible. Then we hate ourselves for failing so miserably.

We wonder what their secret to successful living is. Sometimes we are so bold as to ask for their assistance but find we just don't ever seem to fit in. Some of the more callous individuals, who witness us in the throes of one of those incredibly painful "different states," tell us to "snap out of it."

How we wish we knew how to "snap," but like a complex math problem, we can see the problem but have not the vaguest idea of how to reach that neatly printed solution at the end. We seem to be missing all the steps in between.

In a desperate search to find the missing steps, we seek out a potpourri of therapies and self-help groups; but neither tranquilizers nor antidepressants nor any of the many therapists we contacted knew the steps to take.

We never even made it to step one until that day back in 1983 when, for the first time, a psychiatrist offered us the slightest bit of hope.

We took our first step when the problem was identified, and with that came an understanding of how all our symptoms were related to each other.

We have taken many steps since that cold, sad, and yet hopeful day back in November, 1983. The therapy ultimately ended in disaster as the therapist didn't realize what a bumpy ride it was going to be for both of us. There wasn't much information in those days, so we all had to "wing it."

Ultimately, the therapist ended up getting in over her head and became too overwhelmed with what she heard. She began to unravel. The closer we came to the core of the need to disassociate, the more painful it became for both of us.

We had never given up on our wish for the two story house with the white picket fence. We had thought that once we were an adult and "in charge of our life," we'd make these wise and wonderful decisions and we'd never allow ourselves to be abused again.

How wrong we were! We ended up marrying a man so similar to our Dad that it was horrifying. We found ourselves, once again, in an extremely abusive situation. Only this time, we all felt we were totally to blame. (In our wisdom we had married a man who, like our father, agreed with that judgment.)

As in most abuse, it was an extremely insidious situation, a continuous wearing away. It began with a gradual escalation of the abuse, a slap here and there, a continuous undermining of our almost non-existent self-esteem.

Slowly, my physical and emotional self began willingly to accept the abuse, then to agree with the perpetrators (parents, husband) that we indeed not only deserved all the abuse, but much worse.

The final step was isolation and threats of worse abuse should we ever tell anyone about the abuse.

Soon, we became "comfortable" with the abuse because that is all we had ever known. We continued to protect ourselves in the same method we had learned since childhood, dissociation.

Dissociation would ultimately result in self-abuse, which offered us life-preserving relief from total annihilation. Our self-abuse was not meant as a bid for attention or a cry for help or an attempt at suicide. It was a little death to prevent a bigger death.

After we came out of the self-abusive disassociation, we felt terribly angry at ourselves for hurting us. The self-hate became an almost unbearable burden. No amount of disappointment and/or criticism from others regarding the self-abuse could match our own self-loathing.

We were caught in a vicious cycle. Our life became one continuous struggle for mere survival.

Individuals outside an abusive situation have great difficulty in understanding why the person doesn't just "get out of the situation." They end up blaming the victim for not acting, after all, there *are* several options available.

But what they don't understand is the fear involved in making any decision. No amount of intelligence is enough to counteract the constant fear that an abusive life situation brings. The mere survival condition leaves one living moment to moment: *There is no future—only the present. How are we going to get through this moment alive?*

Because of these factors, one doesn't have the ability, mental strength, and in many cases, the physical health to explore options that appear so obvious to others. One is left not only feeling helpless, but eventually hopeless.

Before escaping this bind, one must solve the matters of finances and finding an understanding therapist who knows how to treat dissociative MPD.

Even today there is, sadly, a tremendous amount of stigma attached to "being in therapy." Treatment for drug addiction/alcoholism is applauded but our society has yet to applaud treatment for any "mental disorder."

In My Own Words

By Libby K.

I can't speak for other multiples, only myself. Multiplicity is pain. It is about bearing unbearable pain. The kind of physical and emotional agony that kills. It is never loving or being loved, never accomplishing, never being good enough, not belonging. It is despising oneself. It is wanting to die and yet not dying.

Multiplicity is full of death. It is viewed as a creative way to avoid madness and death, but there IS death. The abusers caused innocence, childhood, abilities and self-respect to die. The creative process, the overwhelming necessity, and the ability to dissociate took the young human's childmind and split it asunder.

The body lived by burying pain and horror within the minds/hearts/ memories of splintered persons dwelling within the one body.

But we are walking dead persons, separated from feeling by having no feelings, tortured by memories unpredictably surfacing and sinking, stuck in the unfathomableness of time, because time is not continuous or logical.

You may think, "I have pain. What makes a multiple's pain different?" Actual experiences may not be printed, so I will use visualizations all should be familiar with. Look at some of the old newsreels of concentration camp survivors, see the piles of withered flesh pushed by bulldozers. How does it make you feel? Stand next to a pregnant cat smashed flat on purpose by a truck, her unborn kittens flung bloody all over the road. How does it make you feel? Picture the skin hanging in sheets on Hiroshima's children. How do you feel?

Do you want to close your mind now?

Do you want to read another article instead of this one?

Treatment for multiplicity is hell. Of interest to therapists, we may seem "fun." But we live in a hell where everything hurts. The well-seasoned therapist knows the turmoil stirred up during therapy sessions, yet copes and does battle anyway. I would have others know how incredibly difficult the therapy process is. Not fun. Not games. A battle to the end against the huge strangling, struggling dragon in our minds. A battle without armor or sword, only with fleetness of foot and thought to avoid the searing heat of the dragon's fire. Together therapist and patient enter the terror of the mind's forest, the dragon's lair; to attack, then retreat, attack again, run away, hide, attack and retreat . . . each time bruised, scorched and brutally exhausted. Never beaten.

Each of us fights our dragon in our own way and time, with the help of our therapist. I would have others know the intensity of that work, the stakes involved and the toll on daily living and coping that the struggle demands.

Multiplicity is endless sorrow. Creative enough to split, then creative enough to create. All music, art, writing, science is creation. Even love is an act of creation. To suddenly wake up with half of one's life gone—how to measure the sorrow at what was lost, perhaps forever?

I would have others know how even the smallest kindness, the softest, seemingly meaningless touch of a hand, can actually mean the difference between life and death.

I would have others know the special place our therapist occupies in our heart.

I would have a rethinking of the transference principle in psychology as it refers to multiples. Where else has an abused, fragmented multiple known caring, concern, tenderness, protection, a timely kick in the butt? If that is not love—what is?

I would have therapists know we exist from one session to the next and that the relationship, though tested and retested, is precious.

After integration and new perspectives, different matters may be of importance. For now, while still in therapy and struggling, I want others to know our agony, the depth of our sorrow, the intense nature of the therapy process, and the inestimable value of the therapeutic relationship.

I want others to take an unflinching look at the reality of our past and present lives and be willing to stretch out a hand. That hand might, in the moment, mean the difference between being able or not being able to continue battle against the dragon.

Seeking an End to Abuse

By Sarah F.

Many do not want to hear about the unspeakable horrors I have seen and heard, of the evil that is truly in this world, of the ABUSE. It makes them queasy, uncomfortable, unsure. Their eyes seem to glaze over. It is much easier to focus on the results of ABUSE. Tell people you are a multiple and they are fascinated. Their imaginations unwind into fantasies of Eve, Sybil, Dr. Jekyll and Mr. Hyde, or demons and exorcism. The stuff movies are made of. Even so, multiples heal. But the cycle of abuse with its ramifications and ugliness remains firmly in place.

As long as this present attitude abounds, there will continue to be multiples, because there will continue to be ABUSE. ABUSE we permit, by listening but not hearing, by talking but saying nothing, by not believing because it is unpleasant.

If only those rose-colored glasses would fall away, if only the souls of the unabused might suffer, for only a moment, some of the enormous pain survivors feel, just perhaps, the real culprits THE ABUSER and THE ABUSE would stop. Perhaps then the overpowering, destructive results of ABUSE would be eased, and no terrified child would cry silently alone. In time, no one would have to ask, "How do I know which one you are?" "Is this you?"

Just perhaps.

3

SKEPTICS

When I was first diagnosed, I was a mess. If I could have known that I would lose all but one of my friends and alienate other people, I might not have shared the diagnosis so freely. —Aleda

Doubting Thomases

By Robin H.

I wish I had known that the diagnosis of MPD was going to be met with so much skepticism, not only by laymen but also from the psychiatric community.

I read that a 1986 survey found seventy-eight percent of therapists who treat Multiple Personality Disorder had encountered intense skepticism about MPD from fellow professionals. If therapists are encountering skepticism about the disorder, just think what those of us who are diagnosed with MPD are getting.

Not only have I experienced skepticism from other therapists, but also downright rudeness! I have had to be hospitalized several times because of my disorder. Many of the doctors which I and the "others" have encountered told me that my diagnosis was incorrect, my doctor did not know what he was talking about, I was lying, looking for attention, and just wanting to be fashionable.

85

This type of skepticism and disharmony within the psychiatric community almost made me want to hide the evidence of the disorder. That's falling back into the same pattern of secretiveness which I was trying to overcome.

I've put my trust in my doctor regarding the diagnosis of MPD. I try to support those organizations which educate both laymen and professionals in understanding MPD. I'm learning not to become so upset by these "doubting Thomases." A final word on this matter . . . I am *not* an "attention seeking hysteric" but rather an individual who currently has twenty-eight others inside. We are all trying to get things "together" so all can live as one in harmony—no more, no less.

Hiding From Mysel(ves)

By Celeste P.

I wish I had known at the outset, not to be afraid of the label Multiple Personality Disorder. I thought with such a label, I had yet one more thing to hide. At the time I was unaware of just how much I was already hiding. I was not *that* sick. I was just depressed and suicidal.

Then one day, one of my alters contacted my psychiatrist. "It had to be another patient's letter, not mine," I argued. "It's not signed. Why do you think I wrote that letter?" I asked my psychiatrist. Soon I became aware of mysteriously written letters, clothing, trinkets, drawings, and other strange items that I had no way of accounting for.

My mind began to whirl. *Oh! Suppose it is true? Another Sybil? Me? What am I to do? I do not remember anything bad. Nothing bad like Sybil happened to me. I'm just depressed that's all. I look like everyone else in my school,* I said to myself defensively. *I don't see anything, or any people who are not there. So how can these doctors say I'm a multiple? Everybody forgets things now and again. That is no proof, they're mistaken. If I give them time they'll give me another diagnosis. My parents were right; these doctors, my psychologist and my psychiatrist, just want to bleed me for money.*

Perhaps if I did not have any preconceived knowledge about Multiple Personality Disorder, I could have accepted this diagnosis sooner and perhaps engaged more fully with this very intense, difficult therapy. Instead, I fought to be as normal as possible and deny the existence of my alters.

All of my life I have heard voices, but I thought everyone did. Most of the time I thought it was my inner voice speaking. But then I began to listen to the voices and the conversations. I wish I knew then that I was not crazy. I thought I was going to have to hide all this from the world forever.

Now my life makes sense in light of the information that this diagnosis provides. No wonder I got in trouble when I did not do anything—or so I thought. No wonder it seemed I had not learned major chunks of material in school. Perhaps too, this was why some of my friends would stop talking to me and in some instances end our friendships.

Who is going to believe that I have Multiple Personality Disorder? Not my parents, not my closest relatives, *Nobody*. Why would anybody believe it? Or worse, what if they do? Will anybody want to be friends with a Sybil-type person? I would be afraid of me if I were my friend. How can I ask outsiders to understand, when I do not know how myself?

Betrayal

By Grace

I remember the day I was diagnosed with Multiple Personality Disorder. I cried, "No! This can't be!" But inside my desperate hurting was a recognition. I had been trying to find answers to my emotional pain for years.

But now the disbelief and denial I face *with* my diagnosis are much more painful. For friends, professionals and family to deny my reality is much more a rejection of me than before . . . during my search.

Some of my long-term friends felt betrayed by my new diagnosis. One friend said she felt as if all our times together as young women must have been counterfeit. I face her fear of me and it hurts.

I go into a hospital, stay for several weeks. I meet with patients who are hostile, unbelieving, condescending, *fearful*. Because I will not deny the people within their time "out," I often face rejection.

Because I will not deny my disorder, I am subject to gossip and fear. Friends who play with the children "inside" can often be guarded. They are unsure if I can be trusted to take care of children, do jobs, have a coherent conversation. I find myself being constantly patronized. And yet, I am so very needy of their care!

Even the psychological system I go to for help has a tendency to patronize me. My "team" of psychologist, psychiatrists, psych nurses, and social workers make decisions about my life without the most important member of the team's input . . . ME. I wish I had known that people with MPD often lose the respect of friends and colleagues. I know that they are scared . . . but certainly no more than I. Each new revelation brings me and the people within pain and grief. My profound wish is for respect and admiration for our tenacity, our intelligence, our creativity as well as the enormous odds we face each day.

I attend graduate school at a very prestigious university. Prior to my diagnosis, the grad school dean and I would often joke and talk. He was friendly. Since my diagnosis one-and-a-half years ago, he has not looked at me once. He has ducked his head and looked away. Now that I am armed with my truth, I face rejection and that is painful.

But it is not all doom and gloom. In many ways I feel closer to who I am than ever before. Knowing what was wrong with me was necessary before I could begin to heal. I am more sure of myself now. I know what is causing the pain and I am learning to reassure the children within that what is past *is* in the past. I am learning what safety means for the first time in my life.

Many people chafe at "labeling" someone with a psychiatric diagnosis. For me, the "label" gave me freedom to grow towards health. I am an informed consumer/patient.

NOTHING (not even my suspicion) could adequately prepare me for my diagnosis of MPD. It was like a jolt of electricity. But I am reminded that, although dangerous, electricity has the power to light the darkness and I AM grateful for that.

I wish that I had known that the mental health field was not prepared to deal with individuals with Dissociative Disorders and MPD . . . that very few even believed in the diagnosis.

I also found that my friends did not believe. As one said, "I don't think you have MPD. Granted you're different every time I see you—but you are still the same old Patty." —Patricia M.

I wish I had known that I would lose some close friends who couldn't handle my disorder. I wish family and friends could better understand the notion of reliving (abreacting) the experience of abuse.

When I take back/relive the experience (memory, feelings, images of being raped at age seven), it really does mean that I felt raped today when I relived it—even though, in reality, it happened over twenty years ago.

I would like them to know that their strength adds to my strength. Their willingness to bear witness to a very complex disorder and complex treatment keeps me going when I would rather die than go on with this process. It is so painful, consuming all my courage and hope. In one article that I read, they referred to MPD as a disorder of hope. I would strongly, adamantly agree. —Alice O.

Vanishing Friends

By Vickie G.

These past fifteen months have been filled with heartache upon heartache as I have watched friends fall away due to fear and ignorance.

It is so important that people know more about MPD. Being a multiple doesn't make me weird, crazy, or harmful.

If friends and family could grasp how horrendous violent acts of sexual abuse are for a child, maybe they could imagine why that child's mind looked for escape from the pain and terror. Many of my friends have become alarmed and afraid, not knowing what to do or say anymore. Many have stopped coming around or inviting me over. Very few are close anymore . . . which is ironic because I've always had this MPD and they just thought I was moody! People can handle moody.

They need to know the pain of isolation they can cause, the loneliness and misery of being misunderstood. We shouldn't be feared or held as a comparison to Dr. Jekyll and Mr. Hyde.

Friends need to know it's ok to ask questions. It's ok to express their confusion and to clear up misunderstandings as soon as possible. For me, I *want* to talk about what goes on inside. I *need* to express myself. I *want* to know what others think about the way I am. It hurts to have people drift out of my life due to fear of the unknown.

I am willing to help others become more comfortable with my

"parts." I will explain all that I am able to and I am not offended when people ask questions or make "multiple" jokes (usually!). The friends I do have now, ironically, are survivors of child sexual abuse. Since they know firsthand about trauma and dissociation, they seem to be able to look at MPD with much more understanding and empathy. Without their support, I'd be a basket case.

I hope that by educating friends, family, professionals, and the general public, we can dispel the myths and fears around MPD. Living with MPD is hard. It wasn't fair that I had to suffer the first time as a little child. It certainly isn't fair that I must now also suffer as an adult from the "stigma" associated with MPD and incest.

It has been my experience that MPD is regarded as a "freakish" situation. Even though I talked to very few friends about my disorder, most reacted with morbid curiosity. "What happened? How did it happen? Who did it?" Very seldom was anyone at all interested in how it felt, and *that* is what I ached to release most. I do understand their fascination with the disorder, but I need my friends to get past that fascination.

By the time we are able to converse with a friend about what has happened to us, how we dealt with it, the insecurity, and the overwhelming feelings associated with the discovery of the disorder, we need a friend who is willing to learn about the disorder on their own. I often feel like a "public information person," educating my friends—I just need someone to listen. —Carol T.

The experience of other selves is very hard to believe. Any doubt, questioning, or unbelief from the therapist strengthens our own denial. —Judy W.

Precious few psychotherapists even believe MPD exists! *All* of the previous therapists we have gone to labeled us falsely as schizophrenic.

Multiples should always have a safe place, where they can dissociate without the various alters being told, "You're all Amy!" or "Knock off the big act!" I don't have that with anyone outside of my doctor and one friend. —Aleda

I would like therapists (the ones that don't believe in MPD) to know that *WE* are real. We aren't figments of anybody's imagination. We aren't making anything up. I would love to say that I imagined the abuse and my alters, but that doesn't explain the way my life has been up until now.

To the therapists who do believe and already work with MPD clients, I just want you to know that I appreciate your caring and hard work and patience. Being a multiple for me carries a lot of anxiety and fear of being rejected by people. Even though other people are afraid of my pain, my memories, my anger, or just my MPD, my therapist has never shown any kind of negative reaction toward us. I hope all therapists have similar relationships with their MPD clients. —Terry J.

Our Right to Live

By Peggy J.

The hardest part of this diagnosis is that so many "professionals" don't believe in it or say it isn't valid. We spend a lot of time trying to protect ourselves (or conceal ourselves) just so we can exist.

If more psychiatrists, psychologists, therapists and counselors would just accept what is right in front of their eyes, then their acceptance would spread to doctors (MDs), employers, church people, etc. The diagnosis is not always so debilitating that we cannot function at work doing professional jobs. But thanks to rejection and invalidation, so much energy has to be spent hiding that it can affect job performance.

If a person diagnosed with MPD loses her job, without the financial support of a husband, she enters a vicious circle of inability to pay for therapy, becoming disintegrated, needing aid from the government, and often being ineligible for anything, simply because the diagnosis is not accepted.

Too much of my early life was spent begging for the right to live, to not be killed, to be able to eat, to not be raped, beaten, choked, or cut. Now it seems as if, again, we have to beg for the right to live, especially after having become involved with the system. I wonder why we can't be helped back to life instead of hindered?

Educate, Educate!

By Kathy A.

We have been to the hospital three times and that is where the ignorance is especially hard to deal with. Hospitals are scary enough, considering the majority of us are under the age of fourteen.

On our first visit, our five-year-old was frightened and crouched on the floor. She was told to get up and stop acting like a baby. She is a baby and has been severely traumatized. To get more hostility from adults (when it should have been reassurance) just reinforces her beliefs about the world.

Another time, one of the mental health techs told us he wished he could act like different people when he was "upset." We don't "act like" anyone other than who we are. We are all individuals and we each cope with life as ourselves.

Others thought that MPD began for us at the age of forty. They do not understand it began early on, not when we were diagnosed. Each one of us came to cope with our "world" in our own way, to help us all survive just a little bit longer.

At one point after a hostile alter appeared, we were taken to the hospital by police at our doctor's insistence. Because the police and hospital staff initially saw nothing wrong, and did not understand how many they were dealing with, they became lax. They did not take adequate precautions and we were all at risk. The staff must do what the multiple's doctor asks, even if it is hard for them to make sense of it, even if they don't understand.

As time has gone by our doctor has been educating staff about MPD.

For the multitudes of undiagnosed people with MPD, I hope that day is coming when all professionals will possess a deeper understanding of the signs and *reality* of multiplicity. *It could be a matter of life and death.*
—Vickie G.

I wish I had not been misinformed about the diagnosis within my job. This is sad, because I am a mental health worker. MPD and Borderline Personality Disorder are used interchangeably at the hospital where I am employed. MPD patients are not treated with respect and they are rarely believed. —Anne C.

Most of all we need help and understanding, not people saying that we are putting on an act to get attention. Being a multiple isn't easy by any means. We live too many lives. —Will R.

I wish I'd been told upon diagnosis that the road to a very illusive point of integration would be paved with health care systems, facilities, and staff that, at the very best, are extremely cynical.

I wish I'd known about the expensive treatment facilities and under-qualified therapists, as well as the intense pain of reliving the past, which we would endure on our journey toward wellness. —Sharon A.

I have been in five hospitals for eight months, and even though my diagnosis went along with all my records, the staff and therapists in many of these places did not understand. I was put in restraints several times because of the personalities.

Then I became afraid that if the staff did not understand, how would the world outside be able to?

I was out of the hospital nine days and attempted suicide.

Thanks to the perseverance of my therapist, I am still here today. But suicidal thoughts are never far from my mind.

Right now she is the only one I feel safe enough to allow my alters to talk with.

Hopefully, others will understand and I will be able to find my place in this world.

I am so thankful that my therapist cares. —Linda K.

Your Co-Worker Could Have MPD

By Suzanne D.

My greatest wish is that there was more acceptance of Dissociative Disorder diagnoses among mental health professionals. Contrary to some survivors, I feel strongly that this IS a "disorder." If it were simply a very creative response to horrible circumstances, then I wouldn't be overwhelmed so much of the time with feeling suicidal, profoundly depressed and wishing to harm myself. Since there is so much skepticism within the field of mental health regarding even the occurrence of this disorder, I find that in a long list of deep secrets, the fact that I suffer from MPD is just one more.

I am a mental health professional. I work in a supervisory position on a locked unit in a major city. Considering my recent diagnosis (just one year ago . . . after the typical seven or so years in therapies with varying diagnoses), I feel in an extremely precarious position. My "clinical" interest in the Dissociative Disorders is well known on my unit and I am asked for my advice, asked to give presentations, etc. It has become increasingly difficult to comply with requests for educating my staff, considering my personal issues with MPD.

I manage work quite well with the assistance of one other alter. The rest are not appropriate to the setting and have agreed to "not go to work" with me. My peers at work still think "THOSE PATIENTS" are bizarre, do very strange things constantly, switch with rapidity, and are out to manipulate the world. Sometimes I'd like to tell them that I have MPD just to see the shock on their faces at how "well I get by." But I feel it will be many years before MPD and other Dissociative Disorders are accepted as widely as some of the favored diagnoses we now use.

The sad thing is that when clients come in who are obviously having dissociative problems, they're given another diagnosis and sent out the door without ever receiving the specific treatments that might help them to escape the mental health system and lead happier lives.

So what do I wish therapists knew about MPD? That one of their colleagues could very well be suffering from it. That it crosses all lines of wealth, profession, level of functioning.

MPD could be your co-worker's problem . . . or your own.

Coping with the "Rarity" of MPD

By Leslie H.

I am a graduate trained mental health professional with many years of experience with therapy, both as a client and as a service provider. Until the fall of 1989 my knowledge about MPD was scant. My understanding of the prevalence and the wide variations in the intensity of symptoms associated with a clinical diagnosis of MPD was quite limited. I thought it was quite rare, and always accompanied by the extreme disruptions in functioning manifest by Eve and Sybil.

In the fall of 1989, I had been in individual therapy for a year, including eight weeks as an inpatient, with a psychiatrist whom I did and do hold in the highest esteem. She's warm, wise, and witty. She is flexible, creative, and open to new perspectives. She is also on staff at one of the nation's most prestigious psychiatric hospitals. Many of her colleagues at this facility are well-known experts in the area of MPD. She has worked with MPD clients while covering for colleagues; but the idea that MPD might have anything to do with me did not occur to either of us.

Then I joined an incest survivor's support group (while continuing in individual therapy). The group leader was a specialist in MPD. The suggested reading list she gave group members included *Sybil*, which I had read years before, and several similar books which I'd never heard of (*When Rabbit Howls*, *The Minds of Billy Milligan*, and *Prism: Andrea's World*). I read them all. The group leader encouraged "communication with the inner children," and within a month my journal had a section called "The Dialogues." Three "children" and two "adults" chattered and argued with each other on paper. Each one had her own name. Each child was strongly associated with a particular emotion: one was angry, one was sad, and one was happy and playful. The adults represented an intellectualizing coping personality devoid of emotion and, one with the capacity and desire to experience and incorporate all the parts.

I gave copies of the dialogues to my psychiatrist. When I asked her at this point if I might be a multiple, she said, "True clinical MPD is very rare." A few weeks later I had a consultation with one of her colleagues, who is a well-known specialist in MPD. The purpose of this consultation was to explore the idea of hypnotherapy, which my own doctor does not practice. I was astounded to leave this 50-minute session with a "definite" MPD diagnosis.

Six months have elapsed since this event. I've changed many of my thoughts about MPD during this time, and I expect I'll continue to form new ideas. At this point, there are two things I'd like to communicate about my experiences and feelings to date.

1) It was an enormous relief to me to have an explanation for the uneasy blank spots in my past and current life. I think we're doing many people a grave disservice by restricting the DSM-III-R diagnosis of

95

300.14 to the Eves and Sybils of this world. I think it would be far more useful to regard this diagnostic category as a spectrum, or continuum, of symptoms and severity of impairment. I hope the mass media literature will expand to include accounts that are not as extreme as the experiences of Sybil, Eve, and The Troops of Truddi Chase.

2) A month later I felt terror. I believed it was absolutely necessary for me to get much, much worse before I could have any relief. During the decade before my diagnosis I could count on my fingers the number of times I "really spaced out." Immediately after the diagnosis, I began to "lose time" almost every night. Everything I read and heard about MPD predicted that the path to integration would be a very long and harrowing ordeal. I heard it described by experts as "horribly painful . . . with terrifying and repulsive memories that must be reexperienced in full . . . one of the most difficult therapies a patient can undergo . . . very intensive . . . long-term . . . requires several sessions per week for many years . . . ."

What I absorbed from the literature was that the above were absolutely necessary prerequisites to recovery, and I felt overwhelmed with despair. The next few months were some of the worst of my life.

A turning point came for me about a month ago. I said, through sobs, to my wise and practical psychiatrist "I know I have to feel awful, much worse than I feel now, before I can feel any better . . . but I don't know how much more I can stand. I've been in terrible pain, and in and out of therapy, for nearly thirty years now!"

She told me that feeling bad for a long, long time without relief is not a required part of any recovery process, and that it is not inherently noble or necessary. "Feeling bad just makes you feel bad," she said.

I blinked at her through my tears, and remembered the first time I met her. I felt almost as desperate then as I did at this moment. I had been dysfunctionally depressed for months, and had been crying for days. She was gentle and compassionate, and she said, "We need to work on having you feel better." The way she said this gave me *hope*.

Suddenly the dire prospects of years ahead of awful suffering and gut-wrenching abreactions came into question for me.

I also asked myself if I was resisting or denying. But my life has been quite different since that day. I am still in therapy, and I expect to continue for as far ahead as I can see in the future. However, the horrors of some of my past experiences are no longer the central focus of my present life. I am truly learning to be easier on and with myself.

So, from my perspective, I believe we need more flexibility in our treatment protocols with respect to MPD. My experience was that the prediction of a very long, very painful and stormy treatment process became in some degree a self-fulfilling prophesy, and I think that this can also be a disservice to the MPD client.

At present, I regard myself as somewhere between the DSM categories of 300.14 (MPD) and 300.15 (Dissociative Disorder Not Otherwise Specified). The distinctions are not yet sufficiently clear in my mind. What does stand out for me is the need to present a spectrum of treatment modalities along with the spectrum of symptoms within the diagnostic category.

I hope the mental health profession will continue to explore and expand both the diagnostic criteria and the therapeutic options which may be successful. In this process I hope we will remember to focus on what to *do*, and evaluate our interventions on the basis of how helpful they are in mitigating pain and suffering, rather than splitting hairs about what constitutes "true" clinical MPD.

There are many professional people who do not believe multiple personalities exist. I am here to tell you I fought being a multiple for years but there is no other diagnosis which fits me better. It makes my life make sense. —Beverly R.

THERAPY SUCCESSES

*My major supporter, motivator and guide is
my therapist. He is an outstanding and rare
human being. I am extremely fortunate to have
his expertise and friendship. I can't imagine
(nor do I want to think about) MPD patients
who end up with poorly trained therapists or
worse, therapists who don't believe. That's an
additional burden for patients. —Alice O.*

Therapists should know how very integral consistency is to the successful
building of trust. Trust is *the most vital* issue in treatment. Small things
like being late for appointments, or losing a drawing an alter has made
weigh heavily on the success of a relationship with an MPD patient. If
time is so stretched in your schedule, don't take on a patient with MPD.
If you do, realize this is an articulate, sensitive and probably highly intelligent individual. They might very well be able to do things other patients
can't. —Carol T.

I would like therapists to know:

—How losing time feels. How frightening it is not to know what day
it is.

—That I can't always know what my alters did or said.

—How to hypnotize all my alters when some don't want to be hyp-
notized.

—How to get the alters to tell about the past and how to teach the
alters to trust them.

—How to be supportive of me. —Nancy G.

I would like therapists to know that trust is an underlying issue for most MPD clients. Availability is important, as is making it very safe for personalities to come out and share. Therapists should know that the process of recovery is both agonizing and terrifying. —Marsha C.

I wish my therapist had known advanced hypnosis, abreactive techniques, and the genesis/prevalence of MPD. —Charlie A.

ABC Guides for the Therapishrink

By MaryLou P.

Please know that we worry about *many* things, all at once:

   a) Horrible things happen when therapishrinks go on vacation, go to conferences, or just plain aren't available. We get very upset when you leave us: even for a short time. We like to get a postcard in the mail when you are on vacation. We would like your phone number when you go to conferences and things, but don't give it to us, it isn't good for us. Give us the number of another therapishrink or someone else to call.

   b) Are you going to give up and kick us out?

   c) What are your rules? What happens if an angry alter gets out of control? Will you still let us come back? Please don't change the rules without first discussing it with us.

d) Don't start trying to help us if you aren't going to go the whole way and finish with us.

e) Sometimes we think and feel that it isn't really worth all the time, expense and misery.

f) We can't explain to you how really desperate we feel sometimes.

g) All we want is to get and be all better NOW.

h) We want to be real. (Every therapishrink should have a copy of *The Velveteen Rabbit*.)

i) We wish it was safe for us to tell others about being an MPD.

j) Sometimes we really, really need answers from you—so quit with the questions already. We can't handle them. I know that's the way you were taught to do it—but help us, please!

k) All therapishrinks who work with MPDs should get at least double the amount of vacation time because we are so hard on them.

(Cookies make wonderful therapishrinks when the real thing isn't around.)

l) Every MPD therapishrink *MUST* come complete with a box of crayons and plenty of paper.

The Therapy Relationship

By Jessica T.

We have an enormous need both to be loved and to love, because we were so totally deprived of that in our childhood. It took our therapist a long and painful time to accept a careful expansion of the boundaries of the therapy relationship to meet those needs. She has added some mothering-type stuff and some friendship-type stuff, when the primary needs of therapy allow them, and we have thrived on it.

Specific changes include: safe touch; a delight in small gifts we have brought her, such as flowers, scribbled drawings, poems, and delicate embroidery (basic rule—it's O.K. to spend time and energy but not lots of money; money is for paying therapy bills, not for gifts); her telling us how much our love means to her; her sharing things in her own life, such as favorite recipes; her telling us she loves us (after making sure we understood what that does and does not mean).

Limits in therapy launched a new way of working together. The

Limits drove us nuts from the very beginning. We date the official start of The Limits from August 13, 1985 (nearly five years ago as we write this), but looking back, for the year and a half preceding the first cutback and the setting of The Limits, we often panicked whenever we had to end a session or a phone call, and we got drunk nearly every night in an attempt to manage.

Although we worked on abandonment a lot, and things probably improved (we stopped drinking), the core experience of The Limits as hurtful remained until about six months ago. Then one night she said, "It feels like you're trying to make *me* feel like a torturer."

Then (condensing several weeks' worth of work into a few lines), I (being the alter who is the result of the integration of most of the community) replied "You're right, I am. How can I accept how I felt when I tortured people (which I did), unless someone I respect can also live with those feelings?"

"I don't want to feel those feelings."

"Neither do I."

Sigh. "O.K., what do we do?"

"Tell me what it has felt like to hurt me with The Limits and I'll see if it matches what I felt like when I did stuff to people."

So she did and I did and it helped.

It wasn't a one-time thing; we have spent the last six months "visiting" places (her term), like how it felt to turn off the feelings and no longer be able to give a damn what the victim was going through, and how that made us terrified we were becoming like Mommy (who got turned on watching it).

For us, that was the core of what The Limits were about. If our therapist could turn us away, hang up the phone while we were in pain, then she was just like Mommy. We were just like Mommy. *Everyone* was a monster like Mommy. And *that* was screaming nightmare stuff.

When we finally visited that place, we could see that Mommy and Daddy never got around to dealing with anyone's feelings, and we were different. We and our therapist pushed feelings aside when we were too tired to deal any more *right then*, but we came back to them later.

I know I would never have dealt with the stuff I have if she (our therapist) wasn't willing to go there with us and experience our feelings as hers. She says it's much more than is normally needed for abuse victims. It's very hard for her to put herself in the situations I was in, to feel the rage and horror and self-loathing that I am uncovering.

But because she is willing, we have cut down enormously on the amount of transference and the suicidality. We were also making progress (after a year-and-a-half of almost no progress). Sometimes I don't even need to see her as horrible at all. I come into a session, describe what the next piece is, do it, wrap it up, and go home.

Most of the time the transference is really short—a couple of hours or a day or so. And I'm getting free; the horrendous pain is lessening, becoming sporadic rather than constant. I'm coming to accept what I have done and accept the world's failure to save me.

And I tell her that much of the reason I think the world is O.K. is because a world that has her in it can't be all bad. She gets this wonderful glow when I say things like that and she knows she deserves them.

Therapists should let *us* control sessions, set the pace, make the decisions. The therapist's main job is to help us learn how to feel safe, and how to pace, I think. *Never* doubt us. Model good boundaries. Be prepared that we just can't trust you. We need a large support system. —Rebecca R.

I would like therapists to know how extremely fragile some "parts" can be. I had one part that was determined to rid myself of other parts, and went through some very suicidal phases of therapy as a result. Fortunately, my therapist was fully aware of the situation. He allowed unlimited phone calls during that time, and for several months we talked daily (including weekends and vacations). I am now past that point, thankfully. But, I believe, that I survived (literally)—*and* stayed out of the hospital—because of the unyielding support I received when I needed it. I have read that some therapists limit phone calls. Perhaps that works for some clients under other circumstances. But I *know* I would not have made it under those conditions.

I also would like therapists to know how extremely important it is to help your client feel valued as a person. There is nothing more isolating than feeling like you have a "disorder" that you cannot tell anyone about, except perhaps your closest family members. It feels so lonely to work through something so socially stigmatized. Sometimes the only thing that keeps me going is that my therapist respects me and believes in my ability to get through this successfully. —Lori B.

It is not at all a pretty picture, though it is very much real. —Sharon A.

The Delicate Art of Exposure

By MEs

Although I have been functioning over the years in many different states of altered consciousness/personalities, therapy and the process of exposing myself is extremely embarrassing and emotionally painful.

I hated (and still) hate the question, "How many personalities are there?" This question implies the need for proof. If I cannot give a number, then maybe I don't split off; or maybe outsiders won't believe me. I also felt that if I had a high number of alters then I would have MPD for sure. Now I know the number is insignificant.

At first, I was grateful to find out that I had MPD because I was in therapy for thirty years before I found out what was wrong with me. To find out I had MPD was like finding a key to a locked box. I could not wait to start getting well.

After a while I became extremely frightened as more parts of myself became exposed in therapy. Then I went through the "loss of control" phase. I chose to go to the hospital because parts of me were at war and I was feeling very out of control and was fearful of hurting myself. While in the hospital I began learning about controlling myself/myselves and how to work with my ISH, Inner Self Helper, to work with the core self.

Not all hospitals are helpful to people with MPD. Therapists must be responsible for finding hospitals open to the specific treatment methods for MPD. There is much prejudice among the professional community about this disorder.

The "primal scream" and other aggressive expressions of anger and rage can be dangerous for people like me with MPD. I did my best work in this area through walking, exercise, art (drawing what I was angry and rageful about), writing out my feelings and talking in therapy.

The language used in therapy is vital to recovery. My doctor and my therapist taught me that the closed off parts of myself are "altered states of consciousness" and are all parts of me.

I am one person with many parts, not multiple people. I need to claim those parts of me. I found the term "altered states" cold and without emotional attachment or meaning for me. I learned to say, "My altered state named _____." I used my own word, "MEs," which connotes ownership. ("MEs" means me in the plural form, only applying to MPD.) Or I would also say, "The part of me which likes to be called _____." In this way I own my own behavior on all levels of my consciousness, being responsible for my own recovery.

I am not MPD; I have MPD. I am me and MPD is about my behavior and how I relate to the world around me. When I state I am me, I am referring to my core self and my potential to integrate all of my altered states of consciousness into my core self as a whole, integrated, mature adult.

For me, a better name for my condition would be Multiple IDENTITY Disorder, because I identified myself differently in various situations.

Other questions which provoked fear during early MPD recovery were, "How old are you?" or "What is your name?" I did better with questions like, "Is this someone else?" or "What do you want to tell or show me?" After my therapist would converse with an altered state, saying the name and age became less threatening. Sometimes there was just a description like, "the lady with the red hair."

One of the most difficult experiences was when I'd "switch" and afterwards did not know what I did, how I acted or if anyone knew. It is really embarrassing to be in my forties, but acting like a two-year-old, talking baby talk and sucking my thumb.

I did not understand for a long time that the chattering voices "like tape recorders on fast forward" were my altered states, fighting for core attention, or to have me function in their identity instead of my core self.

It has been necessary for my therapist to repeat things to me hundreds of times. Not only did I (core self) need to have things repeated, but all my altered state parts needed to get the message too. Her repeating has helped to save my life and my sanity.

We each experience multiplicity differently. Each of us who share this body experience multiplicity differently and all multiples experience it differently. We will never fit some paradigm or preconceived notion of how we should act, react, or recover.

By working with a therapist, we can discover together what works and what doesn't, what's helpful and what's not, and most importantly who we are.

We would like therapists to think about this:

1) We are not broken and we do not need to be fixed. We've been hurt. We need to heal from those hurts. Sometimes we may feel broken

but we're really not. The feeling will pass. If you try to fix us instead of supporting our healing, we will resent you. If you tell us explicitly or implicitly that you can fix us, we will be hurt all over again. We will sit back and let you try to fix us. When we don't get fixed, we will leave your office knowing that it is our fault and that we are doomed. This gives us one more hurt to heal from. We already have enough.

2) We are strong people. Our healing is our responsibility. You can help by being supportive, by listening, by making suggestions, by answering questions and by caring. The bottom line is that this is our healing and we are strong enough to do it, with some help.

3) Integration is a choice. We are the only ones who can make that decision for us. No one else has the right to make it for us.

4) We are the experts. Our qualifications are our very survival.

5) We will test you and we will not believe you. With enough time, patience and understanding, however, we might start to trust you. If you talk to us from your heart and not always your head or some text book, we will probably trust you sooner. —Annette K.

When I was diagnosed, my therapist was equally in the dark about MPD. I spent perhaps another six months with him before he found me a doctor who had experience treating multiples. That made all the difference in the world!

I have made more progress in the last year than more than ten years in therapy prior to the diagnosis. Little by little we all are learning about MPD. Many times it is just too much to understand, so our doctor has taken it slowly, explaining the details. —Kathy A.

I wish that counselors knew how important it is to help their patients have the support of others as well as themselves. A person with MPD does not usually have the basics of everyday "normal" living within them. They need much support and help to cope with everyday life, as well as to deal with the past.

Therapists need to invest more time with MPD patients. I have found that twice-a-week counseling sessions and double sessions have helped me to cope better. Double sessions can be used when needed, at special times or on a regular basis. I have also found it helpful to tape each session (so that I can listen to it later), for often I cannot remember what has occurred in the session.

MPD is usually a very confusing experience for the patient and leaves them questioning their sanity. The therapist needs to strengthen and support the patient as well as to accept unusual behaviors without being judgmental. This support and non-judgmental approach has helped me to cope with my own dissociation. —Louise H.

Therapists: when working with abuse survivors, make sure you use the words "done to you" rather than "happened to you" because that phrase tends to minimize the degree of abuse. Accept what is said even if it may seem to contradict something said previously. Each personality views the abuse from his/her own perspective.

Be careful when you mention God. Some do not see God as loving; some do not see God at all; some have had God used against them, not exclusive to ritual abuse.

I'd caution all survivors and therapists about falling into the trap of thinking that the personalities are demons, and, therefore, can be "cast out." Each personality is more a positive creation of a higher power than that of a negative power.

Know that sometimes a person or alter feels something but doesn't know exactly what to call it (upset, mad, angry, enraged). Explain that there is a difference, if only by degree. Many know only hurt and anger. All need positive feedback, not more rejection. —Jo Anne M.

I would like therapists to know that I continually doubt and question the diagnosis.

Also, being in contact with other multiples via group, publications, or tapes is something I want. I gathered a great deal of help from learning or reading about how other multiples use their multiplicity in healing. —Marcia L.

Therapists and hospital staff should learn as much as they can about MPD. They should treat each alter as an individual—allow them to talk about why they are there and respect each one's presence. When they have finished talking they should know how to get the host personality back, and explain everything that has happened while that alter was out.

Fortunately, my therapist, upon learning that I was MPD, has attended every conference in the area to learn as much as possible on how to help me. I, for my part, explain as much as I can of what I am going through. As of this writing, I am not co-conscious but we are working with hypnosis in order for me to find safe places.

I'm especially grateful that my counselor helps me be patient with myself as I grow. —Linda B.

Patience and Acceptance

By Cathy F.

It is very important for therapists to be patient and be ready to accept what the MPD person tells them. We already doubt ourselves so much that only unshakable belief on their part will gradually allow us to trust the truth inside.

Many of the images or memories which float to the surface are fantastical. Alters may be the opposite sex from the body; they have various ages; some are a different race and skin color; some are non-human. But they represent us, all inside this one body and inside this one mind.

Our reality goes against everything anyone has been taught to believe is possible. If we are ever to trust our experiences, our memories, ourselves, we must first have a therapist who believes us and reassures us that what we are *feeling* can be true for us no matter how far-fetched it seems to be.

As we gradually begin to believe that our therapist accepts what we tell her, we begin to trust the truth inside and more truths emerge. These truths are the story of what happened to us, how we coped with it, how it felt, how we felt it and what it looks like now, in the present.

Our therapist helps us interpret our experience from a healthy perspective. She helps us learn how to cope with it in a healthy way. Without her belief in our story, and her patience with the time we take to tell it, feel it, live it, and resolve it, we could not begin to transcend those horrors and become whole.

When I was beginning therapy for my MPD, one thing that needed to be explained to me and my alters, was how it worked and how it could happen. I didn't believe it. Some of my alters thought they had bodies somewhere else that they could eventually get to. It was a very confusing time and patience on the part of the therapist was very important. Patience and reassurance. I was so afraid my therapist was going to be like my mother and I didn't want to displease her or disappoint her. Thankfully, she took the time to build a comfortable environment for me so I could learn to trust, not just others, but myself. —Kathleen P.

Accepting a diagnosis of MPD was very hard. My therapist gave me many articles about MPD. I tried to read them, but it was very difficult. I would read and reread them. It was hard to take it all in and my mind (or minds) would only take in so much, the rest was denied and dissociated. (I was good at that.)

There was really nothing else I wanted to know when I was first diagnosed other than the title MPD and a simple explanation. The rest comes with time, work, and awareness. —AMF

When I was first diagnosed, I really had to hunt for MPD information. There was some available, but I couldn't find it. Also we need a book that describes the *many* techniques for working with alters. I use different ones all the time. —Rebecca R.

I would like to be able to rely on my therapist to be with me on this journey and to respect my religious beliefs and needs. —Barbara S.

I was never formally diagnosed MPD. I became aware of others very gradually, after about one year of therapy. I told my therapist about all of us and then began to work on awareness amongst us. I wish I just knew definitively whether or not my experience *is* MPD. —Judy W.

We've read some stuff about multiples that seem to treat the core personality as the "real" person, and the other alters as intruders. Our therapist started out that way, but we (the ones other than the core personality) insisted that we all be treated as a community, a part of the whole.

No single piece of a shattered pot is the "real" pot; every fragment, big and small, needs to be put back in place for it to be whole again.

The original function of the core personality was to push away fragments and memories in order to survive, but he or she shouldn't be encouraged to do that in therapy. Every alter needs a fair share of respect and affection. They all may need help taking turns, including the core personality. —Jessica T.

Therapists should teach other therapists, especially hospital staff, about the nature and treatment issues related to MPD. It's not an overstatement to say that many times when I was hospitalized, my therapist and I had to teach the staff about what to do with me.

Unfortunately, not all hospital staff are open to a patient's direct input into how to plan and carry out treatment. That doesn't even address the problem of what to do with staff who don't consider MPD a legitimate clinical diagnosis.

The first rule of medicine is "do no harm." For MPD patients it could be written "don't abuse them any further." Please refer them, if you feel you can't do the work properly. —Alice O.

The Place of Religion in Therapy

By Grace

I wish therapists could feel more comfortable with discussions about religion and God/ess. After all, many MPD victims are linked to ritual and Satanic abuse. Yet therapists are often afraid to say the "G" word in therapy. I have a really skewed idea of God and need to come to terms with my religious beliefs in order to get well. I want my therapist to be with me in that struggle.

As a seminary student, I often have discussions with other MPD sufferers that they will probably never have with their therapists. They ask me, "Where was God?" "How can *you* worship?" "Does God care?" I struggle with them to find an answer.

Because of a natural reticence on the part of many clinicians, many sufferers struggle with faith issues alone. Moreover, by involving clergy-women/men in the healing process, the clinician finds more support for the victim.

Religious issues strike at the core of my illness. If I am afraid to define my personal theology as it relates to victimization, abuse, and power, then I will not become whole.

In many ways I was abused by religion. Now I must come to understand that that abuse was not only abuse to me, but abuse to valid religious beliefs. I must begin to put God/ess into proper perspective in my life.

Sometimes it may seem like we are running from our work in therapy, but we aren't. We may just not be ready. We do internal work twenty-four hours a day. We work very hard at being "normal." (I hate that word!) We never stop working. —Barbara S.

I wish all therapists knew (as mine do) that MPD is a painful and at times unbearable disorder that causes a person deep anguish, depression and confusion. The best way to describe this is *chaos* and *hell*.

For myself, I need gentleness, kindness and compassion.

Some of the personalities are an embarrassment to share: their behavior, language and memories are horror-filled. I wish therapists knew not to take offense.

Some personalities struggle to share such deep pain that they stutter, cry, or have flashbacks in the telling.

It is exhausting to feel pushed or forced in therapy. I have been fortunate. I have had kindness and gentleness. —Grace Rose

An Inner View of Alters

By Caitlin M.

It seems to me that many therapists simply do not understand that the alters are both a part of and separate from the main personality, and need to be treated with separate respect. I have seen so many therapists treat the alters they liked nicely and the others disrespectfully—as if they were not as full a part of the person.

Therapists don't seem to grasp that when they are talking to the "center," they are being watched by many other eyes, and what is inoffensive to one alter may infuriate another.

Nor do many therapists understand that "time" is fluid, distorted, and warped in many alters, so that past is present, or the present has never been.

I wish therapists realized that with MPD one lives mostly in a variegated inner world which may have wars and disagreements which spill over into the outerworld. There is not a single "I" controlling daily life. Each alter must be dealt with on its own terms.

Above all, I wish therapists understood that we have MPD because of severe abuse, and that alters need to come to loving cooperation and—in my opinion—integration. No therapist should encourage separateness.

111

Building Trust Together

By Eliza K.

The first thing we need to hear is that we're not crazy. You'll probably have to say that a lot before we'll hear you and a few thousand more times until we believe you. Not only does it sound bizarre when you explain it to us, it has felt even more so—often for years!

MPD didn't have a sudden onset like intestinal flu and it won't go away in twenty-four hours with hot tea. It probably won't ever go away completely, but, unlike the flu, we can function day-to-day and learn to tolerate, if not actually enjoy it!

We can be independent, creative, competent people who function quite well in society. We don't have to think of ourselves as handicapped.

We also need to hear that by virtue of being multiple, we are strong (after all, we have survived), and we are intelligent. It's a tremendous boost to be able to regard ourselves positively when we have to face a truckload of negative memories.

MPD didn't happen randomly. We made a choice, however subconsciously, to protect a vulnerable and sensitive child, which means we triumphed over the adult(s) who hurt us.

Help us to see that *why* we were hurt is not nearly as important as the fact that the children we were at two, or five, or twelve had more sense and better judgment than the adults who caused the pain.

Even though we may have an intellectual understanding that it is futile to resolve the reason *why* this condition affects our lives, emotionally we continue to look for the fatal flaw that made us a target. You will need to keep helping us place the blame where it truly belongs.

It's not easy for us to accept that MPD was our choice, so we need to hear that often as well. It's much easier to work with the condition instead of flailing at it. MPD was a friend whose fierce protection is no longer needed.

Expect us to try your patience with our resistance to Mixed Emotions. We've lived with black and white so long that shades of gray are only good as colors for cats and rural mailboxes. We may typically be pleasant and agreeable in therapy, but the day we have to grapple with the dread M.E. you may wish you'd gone into the used car business. We won't be very sympathetic. We will probably hold you solely responsible for creating the monster.

We don't do anger well either, so you might have to tell us that we are indeed angry. Wait a moment, and then announce that furthermore, we are probably angry at you. Therapeutically, it's a golden opportunity.

Not only are emotions a perplexing maze of alien design, many of us find sex equally disturbing. For many of us it isn't even safe to discuss, let alone do, and God Save The Queen when we start to remember the role it played in our young lives.

You may have to be superhuman in your compassion, persistence, and skill just to keep us in the same room with the subject; and you'll need to be matter-of-fact, patient and knowledgeable, because we're not.

We are, however, masters at changing the subject, and will put our greatest charm and effort into subtly luring you toward safer waters.

Our discomfort with sex is probably in direct proportion to its function in our multiplicity; so, although it's unlikely we'll be grateful if you point that out—we *do* have to talk about it. Besides feeling acute discomfort, many of us become very frightened when the subject of sex is introduced, and we may not know why. We're aware that little, if anything, in our adult sexual experience could have contributed to this overwhelming panic. So we are embarrassed about the level of our distress, and wish we could disappear into the seat cushions.

How you handle this most difficult subject may well determine the course of therapy. We don't want, but very much *need* for you to be forthright, explicit, honest, and accepting. Then there's the matter of touch. I believe we need to be touched. You may be the first loving (yet non-sexual), supportive, caring person in our lives. We may have trouble just figuring out what *that* means!

Many of us can intellectualize with you until the cows come home. We can have profound, even brilliant exchanges without stirring up any of those pesky emotions . . . but take our hand in yours—even for a moment—or give us a friendly hug, and wordlessly, like the walls of Jericho, our barriers come tumbling down.

We can defend ourselves with a barrage of words, but we have virtually no defense against gentleness.

Many of us are hungry for that kind of nurturing, but we've forgotten how to ask for it, if indeed we ever learned. But then, I suppose, if we had gotten enough of the right kind of touching, we wouldn't be multiples.

We'll probably need to talk about touching a lot, especially when you connect with our internal kids, (some of whom are very young children).

113

Even if the package that contains these kids is 6'4" and weighs 220 pounds, the little ones inside need to be treated as children. Forget that the adult has a Ph.D. in nuclear physics; the kids inside like to color with crayons, play with their food, and sleep with a teddy bear.

Their behavior is probably age-appropriate, however incongruous that may seem to both client and therapist. Your lap may become a two-year-old's safe haven, or a five-year-old might wrap little arms around your neck and demand a story—totally oblivious to the size discrepancy (though the adult they become outside of therapy may not be).

Some of us find the child behavior to be awkward and out of control. We adults need reassurance that you are comfortable with all our selves. The children inside will probably demand some interaction with you, and the younger the child, the greater the need for hands-on communication, since words for them are not a reliable way of sharing. Even older children who do have a facility with language, often do not trust in the validity of words alone.

Would I have wanted to know all of this at the beginning of therapy? Not at all! It was enough to know that I wasn't crazy; that I had made a wise choice as a child to become multiple; and another wise decision as an adult to work toward greater wholeness. And most of all, I knew that I had and still have an intuitive, courageous, and loving therapist who wanted to work with me on this rather incredible journey.

Whether she always knows where we are going, or if she sometimes plays it by ear, her air of absolute confidence assures me that we will, some day, arrive at our destination.

A Note to My Therapist

By Lynn D.

I wouldn't wish my feelings or experiences on anyone, especially on my therapist. Lately, we have been learning more and more about our past, and the pain is intense. In some ways, he shares the burden of our pain. He does not try to own it, he just knows about "being with."

I feel fortunate. My therapist was a good psychotherapist before he knew much about MPD. He was flexible, he cared, and he was still learning and growing. When he first knew he was probably dealing with a multiple, he sought out advice—expert advice—and he continues to get it. He is always ready to learn more. He says he learns from me, and I certainly try to share anything that I learn. And with all this "MPD education," he still trusts his solid knowledge of psychotherapy.

So, what I want to tell *my therapist* in relation to *my MPD* is this:

I appreciate all that you do for me and with me. You are helping me to continue to survive and improve and, slowly, to heal. I know that this is not an overnight process and I am willing to keep working. I know that I must do this work—you cannot do it for me—but what you do makes success more possible.

I also see a parallel. I know that you worked very hard on your own growth and healing. This has allowed you to help us—and many others. I think that is one reward for your efforts. This knowledge is an inspiration; my healing process has already allowed me to give to others, and, by example, you've taught me that this is what life is all about.

I wish my therapist understood how frustrating "lost time" is for me, and what it's like to go through a memory. I doubt that anyone but a survivor can fully understand the pain, the real pain that comes with "reliving" it.
—Diane H.

Multiple Personality: A Patient's Perspective

By Carole G.

"I don't think I'm ever going to get well!"

How many times has any therapist treating multiple personality patients heard that? Probably about as many times as "I am determined to get better!" Confusing, but true. And so it is to the patient. I know, because I am one.

Writings about multiple personality problems and behaviors by knowledgeable people have increased significantly in the past ten years or so. This is excellent! The more psychotherapists who learn to diagnose and treat multiple personality disorder, the better chance a patient has to recover.

Problems and difficulties from the patient's perspective have been generally overlooked. I'd like to present some of my thoughts on the subject.

Electrical resistance

Resistance is a way of life for most multiples. They grow up relying on its value as a protective device. Any possible cruelty is averted by use of this automatic response.

It starts the very first time an abused child is molested or rejected in some way. The first reaction is to resist what is happening. Pain and hurt demand that a strategy be worked out—usually by a baby with no cognitive strengths in place.

A neglected or incestuously raped baby or child has no chance of going to the authorities, or even talking about it. Options necessarily come from elsewhere. But the feeling of resistance to pain remains.

As the child grows, and with continuing trauma, the resistance grows. On the outside this child may seem a meek little lamb. But on the inside there are big fences with lions behind it. The fences are electrified, to make sure the unacceptable feelings of the lions will not emerge.

By the time the psychotherapist is dealing with this patient, feelings of resistance are incredibly strong. Further, they are not fully recognized by the one who has them.

Determined denial

This same baby, whose only avenue of resistance was to cry, found it did not stop the pain, so she turned to denial. In other words, she learned to split off what was so painful, thereby giving it "away."

Resulting dissociation fed into multiplicity under the right circumstances. Having learned the trick, it was easy to do again, and again, whenever it was needed. Soon it got out of hand and happened when not wanted.

This is determined denial. Denial at any cost. Even the multiple who has been in therapy for a long time turns to denial in one form or another. To deny being multiple after three years' therapy is one form. To split off another alter in the face of some stressful situation is another. Denial comes even after heavy abreactive work. It takes time to accept.

Transference transporter

A tricky little device called transference lies at the heart of a therapeutic alliance. This is especially true in dealing with multiples. Flashbacks, memories and abreactions can occur from the smallest trigger. Ideally, the trigger will come from the therapist, and can be worked through in the therapy session.

But all too often, triggering takes place outside the office. The patient is then left to re-dissociate or contend with the leftover feelings of the abreaction. Such is the nature of multiplicity.

Transference for dissociative clients can seem very concrete. The therapist, in mid-sentence, can immediately take on the looks, demeanor, words, and even voice of a perpetrator. The patient might as well have said, "Beam me up, Scotty," because she has gone into abreaction!

This abreaction or memory will finally burn out. But as always, the feelings remain as dusty ashes . . . the kind one cannot quite brush off. What is needed is a handy dust-buster, a therapist willing to commiserate, to assure and finally to convince the patient that what *happened* was awful. *The therapist is not the perpetrator!* Both of you will talk it out until the patient feels safe again.

On paper, this sounds easy, but it takes time.

A further complication takes place if the therapist actually shares many of the same habits and styles as the patient's abuser. It is up to the therapist to continually sort out the differences between himself and the perpetrator. The patient is in no frame of mind to make the distinction. Until the patient understands this, a consistent therapeutic alliance will never be reached.

Rusty trust
Trust is something that has to be built upon, starting from some positive base. Multiples usually have very little historical basis for trust. From early childhood, the toddler learned it was best to stay away from a psychotic mother or a drunken father. Neither could be trusted. Further, none of the painful, disturbing or frightening things that did happen were ever to be talked about.

This results in the family-system institution of denial: whatever is never discussed either never "really" happened, or is of no "real" importance.

Trust between therapist and patient is often slow in developing. The patient's biggest concern is that the therapist not repeat any abuses that have occurred in the past—physical, sexual or mental.

It's also valid that trust is a two-way street. The therapist must convey confidence and trust in the patient's sincerity as she describes thoughts and experiences.

Finally, confidentiality is a must! It helps to reconfirm often that shared information will remain private.

Trust is an extremely fragile thing. It can be crushed as easily as a butterfly.

Angry? Not me!

As a general rule in this society, it is more acceptable to feel hurt than to feel angry. The multiple tends to the hurt position. Because of her experiences and censorship from society, she has learned that in the midst of some horrendous abuse, her very life could be in jeopardy if any word or attitude of anger is expressed. Her anger has been pent up too long. Learning to let it out judiciously and correctly is difficult. Initially, there will be much hesitancy and resistance. Although I have taken several assertiveness training courses, it is continually a struggle to be assertive or angry when the situation demands it.

A "there and then" situation may be slightly easier to work with than the "here and now." Specifically, if the patient transfers angry feelings onto the therapist instead of an abuser, it would help for the therapist to point it out and explain what is taking place. Chances are that the patient would find it more acceptable to be angry with someone not present in the room.

The logistics may seem a little strange, but it gets the job done.

Abreactive shell shock

Fear of the unknown is one of the hardest things anyone has to face. But to an MPD patient, fear can be so overwhelming it can stifle purpose or direction. After going through a particularly unnerving abreaction, the therapist may be feeling positive about the progress made. He may not realize that the patient may be still trying to assimilate what horrific or terrifying memory has shaken her entire being. She may not see it as progress at all.

The therapeutic response to abreaction is to rehash and go over the memory until it loses its negative effect. It is difficult for the therapist to know if and when the negative effect has been alleviated. In trying to please the therapist, the patient will often pretend to accept the abreaction as complete. She will not deal with it but will trance out or switch to an alter who can deal with it.

The client is most vulnerable at this time, and most likely to leave therapy in confusion and fear. Pain, hurt and guilt can be all-consuming.

And in the knowledge of what went on during the abreaction, it is feared that worse might be coming.

When this happens, the patient needs the wisdom and support of the therapist to see what has created trauma in her life. She must continue dealing with it. This takes time that is desperately needed by the patient and can be very beneficial to therapy.

"Fright or flight"

If you have ever put your finger on a hot stove, you have some idea of the reaction that most multiples feel when certain subjects are brought up. It puts them in what I call the "fright or flight" mode. The therapist has to be prepared for either occasion.

In the "fright" mode, the patient will automatically jump into abreaction or a memory of some intensity. It is so rapid that often bodily reactions cannot keep up. It is almost as if one can see oneself putting a finger on the hot stove, but cannot stop. Then the pain or horror comes with the memory but the finger will not come off the stove.

In the "flight" mode, the patient just uses the old standbys of dissociation, trance, or switching to avoid dealing with the stove and the pain it brings.

My guess is that the best way of dealing with the "flight" mode is to turn off the stove at first. Then turn up the heat slowly—basically, warming your way into a memory. It may be that it is not yet time for that memory to surface.

ISH's wishes

ISHs (Inner Self Helper) are among the multiple's most useful alters. They come in many shapes, sizes, and have many differing functions and uses.

Generally, an ISH knows quite a lot about what is going on inside, and so is in a good position to help the therapist. It is possible for some ISHs to stop an abreaction if it comes at a bad time. Some can switch consciousness to different alters if the need arises. But the ISH is able to help the therapist most in knowing what is going on in the patient's mind, in knowing if it is best to work in certain areas at certain times, and in being there when self-abusive behavior is forthcoming.

The ISH is the strongest protector of the system, yet most understand the healing nature of painful abreaction and so allow it to happen for the long-term goal of health. The therapist would do well to listen closely to his or her suggestions.

119

Other things which may seem small but definitely help a patient's frame of mind are: a big smile and welcome when entering your office; treating the patient as a person and not as a problem to be solved; giving as much information as possible about the direction of therapy. Most of all, a positive farewell (physical contact preferred—a hand on the shoulder, a hug, or even a handshake) is needed.

Advice From a Group of Young Alters

By Tina B.

Talk to us like you would any other person you have just met. If you know us, call us by name or number or age. If you want to speak to us directly, call us, we will answer. Be aware that some of us don't speak or understand language too well.

If we switch in front of you, ask who is present and give us time to find out, and answer. Don't bombard us with one question right after the other. If you feel uncomfortable, say so. We respect honesty. Talk to us later.

If you do communicate with us be age appropriate. Use simple sentences for young children.

If you must write things down, ask permission. We get frightened and/or angry.

Many of us insiders are also afraid of other insiders.

If you could help us and yourself to figure out the structure of our system, it will be a help to us and you later on. Don't push! We will become co-conscious by learning about ourselves and the others.

Don't ask for "bad" people to come out until you get to know us. We are afraid of them and you will be too. Ask later, make sure you're safe and we are too.

"Integration" is a scary word. So don't ever throw it around. Use it later when you know us and what might be possible for healing.

In working with us, we sometimes need you to come get us to talk . . . especially the young weaker ones.

Also, know that there are those of us who will be angry if we tell too much, and who will try to hurt us. Pacts or contracts have to be made to insure our safety.

If one of us tells you a story and then you hear the story again, it might be somebody new.

Our traumas are deep and long. If you can't go the distance, please leave us where we are, "buried alive."

I hope therapists realize that MPD doesn't end when we walk out of a therapy session; that we always need much more of their time and attention than is possible. MPD therapy can feel like a never-ending story even though we're reassured that it is curable. For us, the complications of being multiple can be overwhelming as we try to deal with the diagnosis, cope with the "real" world, uncover memories, and manage the symptoms that follow—all while enduring a constant and intense feeling of aloneness.

For us, one of the most difficult aspects is the intense dependency on the therapist(s) which develops. We despise feeling so dependent and this often gets in our way and slows down progress.

And finally, our hope, motivation, and determination to continue rather than give into the agony is kept alive not by the therapy itself, but by the caring we may be lucky enough to receive from our therapists.
—Virginia C.

I wish my therapist understood that each of my "inner children" have different needs and fears and each of them need to be dealt with according to their specific nature.

It is hard, terrifying, and confusing to be one person in body; to know I am an intelligent and capable person but at the same time have thirty-three different voices, all screaming at once and acting things out on my body that I am not even aware of. Sometimes the experience is totally overwhelming and my core adult has trouble controlling the civil war erupting inside.

It is a lonely scary place to be inside of me. Sometimes, you can shut the office door or hang up the phone, but I must take "me" with me. Sometimes it is an awesome task to be with all of me all the time.

I feel so hopeless at times. I need encouragement to go on when I can't see the light ahead.

My inner children and I totally reexperience each memory. I see what is happening, smell the smells, feel the emotional terror, feel the physical pain occurring, sometimes even to the point of bleeding. My body shakes in fear; even my teeth chatter. To me or any of my inner children, the abuse is happening NOW!

121

My inner kids and I need *constant* reassurance that we are NOT CRAZY, that we are believed and, especially, that we are not BAD or DIRTY because of the things done to us or that we were forced to do. We need to be told, "Those were terrible, awful, and mean things done to you!" and that we did not deserve, desire, or cause these things to happen to us.

All of me needs to know that there are some "safe" people who can be trusted and who don't want to hurt us. Not everyone and everything is bad!—Janet F.

Just One Day

By Reane P.

I wish every therapist of a multiple could literally spend one entire day with their patient. My doctor tries to understand and uses her knowledge as best she can to help. But sometimes, when she doesn't intend to, she really stirs things up in the hour of therapy. Then I have to go home and try to function, cope, and do what's expected of me, for another 167 HOURS.

In this time, as I struggle through, I continually project hope to the next session that she can do something to make things better. Usually it's a wasted thought. I feel if she really knew how hard it is, that she would be more cautious on certain issues.

I also wish all therapists would understand the physical pain involved with headaches and some flashbacks. Physical pain makes functioning impossible. I believe something should be done to provide medication more readily and easily.

Obviously, if the client abuses medication, this won't work. However, some sort of contract should be maintained and perhaps a standing order for medication could be left with a family physician or emergency care center for those times when the pain is too intense.

In conclusion, any person, doctor, therapist, spouse, or friend, who knows or deals with a multiple on an ongoing basis, is truly an angel from God. The patience, understanding, and care it demands, makes anyone who attempts working with a multiple a VERY SPECIAL PERSON.

I would like therapists to know that we have feelings, the same as anybody else—we just have more of them! —Will R.

A Multiple View

By Barbara G.

We are capable of doing much more than most people give us credit for. And we like to perform a multitude of duties. We constantly watch each other perform in a variety of ways, although we don't always have control. Most of the time, we do find ourselves overwhelmed with the lists of things "to do." And even though we go through periods of questioning our ability to complete a task, we *know* deep inside the panic is unnecessary. Somehow, someone will take over and succeed.

MPD is like living on a three-layer chess board. You can watch what is happening as people move from level to level. The difference is, no one dies! There are altercations which result in simple demotions or promotions. There is constant action and too much noise. Headaches are horrendous!

(We have built models of this board to show both doctors. They understand that the "three-levels" are there for demonstrative purposes. There are many invisible levels below, between and above the boards.)

There is never enough time with a therapist . . . but understandably that is every patient's complaint. Everybody inside wants some time and *everybody doesn't want the same therapist*. People's communicative skills differ. There are those among us who code-write, speak different languages, cannot hear or speak, etc.

There should be some kind of support group or a drop-in day center for crisis intervention . . . not *hospitalization*. (We are left alone too much.) The threat of being hospitalized prevents us from sharing certain things with our therapist.

There should be more than one therapist. Doctors and therapists need to learn that "two heads are better than one to figure it out." I think that teams of male and female therapists are better able to ease anxiety.

The fact that we are still in therapy after so many negative experiences proves we are desperate. But wanting to get better is not really for ourselves. It is because we don't want our families to suffer. Our true wish is to *be dead* . . . not to *kill* ourselves, just to *be dead*!

Teach us to relax. Hypnosis is very helpful. Although you think we space out easily and can do it all of the time, really controlling this is new to us. We need help learning to relax. It is very frustrating trying to create this new "state" when there are so many people running around and the noise is deafening. Try to remember that everyone has a job and they are always working. We sleep very little.

Trust takes time and building trust is very important. Don't give us medication with unlimited refills. Some of us save medication and do have ulterior motives. They are not so stupid that they can't kill themselves with over-the-counter drugs but some may want to use *your* drugs just to get back at you.

We are *very* sensitive to your moods. Acting nice to an adult alter might produce the feeling of "condescending." Acting abrupt to Wee Ones will definitely be threatening! (We're glad we don't have your job . . . although we think we would be quite good at it!)

Gregory Here!

For Cindy B.

It's Gregory writing this for everybody inside, because I like to help.

My therapist, helps us because she *likes* us and so she is very, very, very honest all the time with us. And when she doesn't like something we do, she tells us because she trusts us a whole lot. *A lot.* And so when we get mad at her (sometimes, but not a lot) we can tell her and she's not afraid or mad. So we aren't either.

Somebody else inside wants to add that it is very confusing and scary being a multiple, so the most important thing is for the therapist not to be confused or scared. Our therapist takes plenty of time and doesn't rush us (and doesn't like us to rush) because she has lots of confidence in everything, so we aren't so scared either. And most important, she believes us and is always on our side and even when she doesn't like what we do, she stays with us on our side and teaches us what to do when we want to make blood. She isn't afraid. She trusts us.

When Caring Counts

By Susan B.

Even though clients, like myself, may readily and frequently deny experiences of MPD, the pain, confusion, and fear we experience are very real.

The experience of abreaction is real. I have been very lucky to have a therapist who understood what was happening to me when I did not. She encouraged me to go through the experiences and learn from them. She also gave me time and permission to stomp my feet and say "I don't want to do this!" always with the understanding that it was important for me to remember the past. While experiencing past abuse so vividly that it feels like it is happening all over again, my sense of security was completely lost, just as it was when I was a child. I depend on my therapist as a base of safety and security during an abreaction. The fear of abreaction is so great that it is very important for the therapist to be that security base. It is important to know that there is someone who will help you make sure you won't get stuck back there.

I hope therapists understand that our crises are very real to us. Although others may look at us and say, "You are sitting on your couch in your own safe home. What's the crisis?" Living through an abreaction means feeling that the threat is right here, right now. The genuine caring and patience of therapists is as important as their knowledge and experience. Fear of being known interferes with therapy. —Stephanie M.

I wish that we had known more about transference when I was diagnosed MPD. It is a difficult thing to understand in the beginning. I was hard on myself and on my doctors and felt miserable about it. I feel that it could have caused me to end therapy. —Kathy C.

Therapy is no piece of cake. It is the hardest work I have ever had to do. Sometimes I get the feeling that people just think I go four times a week to the therapist and we sit and chat about everyday problems. I wish it were that easy. —Diane H.

Being Human

By Susan C.

It is very difficult not to think of ourselves as individuals or separate. We need to be reminded frequently that we are a part of Susan. I also have to keep telling myself that there are other parts of me. Accepting this is accepting the experiences and all the feelings that come with them.

Even for a high functioning MPD patient, the internal work that goes on is very disabling at times. During these times the basics of taking care of oneself need to be reinforced by the therapist and family, just as the MPD patient must practice trusting and asking for help.

We believe that nurturing physical contact is as important as talking. Most children need to be held. So do multiple children.

I do not believe touching is a cure in itself. It is a part of the healing. Hugs upon arrival or departure may be enough connection for some. Yet a handshake may be too much for others since there has already been negative physical contact, a loving touch can be frightening at first—unfamiliar—and then welcomed, thus healing.

I hope you will talk to your patients about being human—just living: life's ups and downs, tears and laughter. Be real to them. Treat them special (they *are* special) without losing or crossing your boundaries. It *can* be done.

And don't forget to listen, listen, listen. Someone inside will almost always tell you what is going on. No matter who shows up, recognize them for who they are. Listen, talk, be and work with them.

I'd like therapists to know that other severe (ritual/satanic) abuse survivors and MPDs can teach and support me more than anyone. I need an MPD support group, a ritual abuse therapy group, or some way to meet and get to know other survivors, in addition to individual therapy.
—Kim B.

Talking Out the Pain

By Celeste P.

At the time I was diagnosed, I had far to go in learning to communicate my feelings and emotions verbally. I was in no way prepared to communicate the bits and pieces of what I now know is memory.

In general, sex has not been an easy subject to discuss. Victims of sexual abuse generally are taught not to talk. In some cases talking—period—meant punishment.

I wish I could have told my therapist from the beginning about everything, but I could not explain how or why it was so difficult for me to approach certain issues.

Sometimes my therapist unknowingly set up situations that seemed to leave me no way out. Even today they feel abusive. My friend, my lifeline, my hope for the future, is asking that I break what has become a law for me. My therapist wants me to talk. Can I trust her? Is this a test to catch me again that will result in punishment?

Since the traumatic abuse it takes to cause someone to dissociate is so extreme, and is kept a secret, the multiple has no idea of what he or she is embarking upon in healing.

The word "integration" does not describe what the individual will have to go through to get there. Many of us are told we have to re-live the past traumas and share the pain; talk about it; understand it in a new light; and understand it wasn't our fault because we were children. Once all of this has been accomplished, we will be able to put the past in perspective so it causes little or no pain.

But what happens when you re-live the harm you personally caused someone else who was as innocent as you once were? What happens when you discover that alters within you hurt people the same ways you were hurt—using the same methods, the same cruelty, and the same hatred?

I so dearly wish I'd had a support system/network available when I was diagnosed. They do exist now, thank heavens! My whole life, everything that kept me alive, the lies I told myself, the distortions—were all vanishing.

My fear of people has increased exponentially. If I had time to meet with other multiples, share their pain, see how others dealt with the different losses and new information, perhaps I would be able to reach out to those people when I'm terrified the most.

So often I am confused about who is *safe*. How do I tell the difference? My experiences—up until the time I was able to *trust* my therapist—eliminated human beings as reliable sources of help and comfort.

I found out that support groups can help in ways that my therapist cannot. Sometimes you need to *be with someone* and that is all. In support groups I found others could understand feelings I could not put into words. Most importantly, I found in a support group the strength to keep fighting to live.

I was able to learn some new ways to approach and look at myself, my alters, my behavior, my problems with denial and saboteurs, and problems with communication with my alters. Some of the people had a greater impact on me than others, some were veterans at talking about certain kinds of abuse, but all were helpful with their experiences.

The Gift of Multiple Friendships

By Susan A.

For individuals with Multiple Personality Disorder, associating with others with the same diagnosis can be a very beneficial experience. Through friendships with individuals with MPD (which I will hereafter refer to as multiples) and a therapy group for multiples, I have received much emotional support. I have also learned much about myself and relationships.

Unfortunately, many professionals in the field of MPD are wary of condoning multiples knowing, and developing relationships with, other multiples. I would like to explain the benefits of friendships among multiples as I have come to understand them.

In order to derive the following benefits, I feel that it is crucial that each multiple be fully invested in their own therapy(ies). This is necessary for several reasons. First, it is essential that each multiple be focused on healing him/herself. Second, a therapist can confront the client should he/she become resistant to doing his/her own therapy work and, instead, choose to focus on "rescuing" other multiples. Third, a therapist is needed to help the client sort through the multitude of feelings that accompany emotional growth and the receiving of "rewards."

Benefit 1: Decrease in shame/Increase in self-esteem

One of the first rewards that I experienced through my association with other multiples has been the lessening of my sense of shame. I had always felt ashamed of the degrading and perverted sexual things that were done to me and that I was forced to do. I had always felt that I smelled, that people knew my secrets, and, therefore, that they could never love me. However, through a group for multiples, co-led by therapists, I met other women who had experienced similarly unbelievable abuse.

It was a relief to know that I had not been the only person to have been repeatedly put through such atrocities. I learned that they too felt that they smelled, that their secrets were branded on their foreheads, and that they were bad and unlovable. I knew that those perceptions were wrong.

Members of my group tried to convince me that those perceptions of myself were also wrong. Over time, I began to see that my self evaluations were as faulty as theirs. I began to trust their more positive perceptions of me and to see myself as a person worthy of love and respect.

Benefit 2: Decrease in "aloneness"/Increase in ability to communicate

It has been very comforting to find that I can express my experience as a multiple to other multiples and be readily understood. They accepted my memories. They didn't shy away from them in horror, for their memories were similarly incomprehensible. They also had a special talent for understanding my embarrassed and cryptic language and art work. I felt empowered as I learned to let go of the burden of guilt and secrecy. As I found ways to share my experiences with other multiples, I became better able to take those same experiences to my therapist. As a result, my therapy progressed much more rapidly and profitably.

Benefit 3: Decrease in misperceptions and self-punishment/Increase in objectivity and care of self

Other multiples have been able to help me evaluate my experiences more objectively. I have often felt that I was the bad one, that I was the one that should be punished; not my abusers. Such thinking was confronted by my fellow multiples. They helped me to understand that it was the small, naive and powerless child of years ago that was abused—not the more able adult of today. They could clearly see that it was my abusers that were to be held responsible for the horrible things that occurred.

As my feelings of self-blame and self-hatred decreased, so did my need to mentally and physically hurt myself.

Benefit 4: Decrease in isolation/Increase in healthy relationships
Until recently, I have been a loner and afraid of letting people become close to me. I feared that they'd learn of my secrets, or that they'd hurt me. Also, I didn't know how to develop a healthy relationship.

Such is also true of most of the multiples I have met. However, through a group for multiples, I have learned that others will accept me (my collective self).

But first, I had to begin to trust them and let my guard down. As our relationships in the group grew beyond the superficial level I had much opportunity and motivation to learn how to offer and/or ask for support; to ask for clarification before jumping to conclusions; to be assertive; to deal with conflicts; to forgive, and much more.

Gradually, I became able to transfer those social skills to non-multiple neighbors and co-workers.

Benefit 5: Decrease in socially destructive behavior/Increase in insight of self and others
My behavior used to be very egocentric. For example, when I cut myself, disappeared without explanation, made suicide attempts, etc., I did so believing that it was my prerogative to do so, for I was only affecting myself. Other multiples in my therapy group believed and acted on that same premise.

However, when the multiples that I had become close to did many of those same things I was definitely affected. For example, I felt worried and powerless when they hinted at suicide attempts, hurt and angered when I saw their self-inflicted wounds, and frustrated when they tested my friendship.

As a result, I came to realize the effect my actions may have had and can have on others.

I also had great motivation to learn how to deal with the overwhelming feelings associated with friends, to draw my own boundaries, and to set limits. (This is where a therapist's objectivity can be invaluable.)

Lastly, I learned that I could turn to my friends for help in discovering alternative solutions to problems that in the past would have led to isolation and self-destructive activities.

In summary, while a knowledgeable therapist is essential in the successful treatment of MPD, I have found that it is the association with other multiples that is a real impetus for growth.

Multiples can act as mirrors for one another. They help translate the cognitive gains, made in therapy, into lasting changes in behavior.

I'm appalled by stories I hear of abusive or incompetent therapists.

I find that we with MPD test boundaries to the limit; I wish therapists were self-aware and courageous enough to help us untangle the hell from our pasts and firm enough to maintain appropriate boundaries.

Sure, I'll manipulate for comfort any way I can; but that leads me back to dependence. Over-dependence can be a real pitfall for therapy.
—Caitlin M.

Guilt and Morality

By Jessica T.

Unlike most abuse survivors, who need help seeing that they are *not* to blame for what happened to them, I think that those who were trapped into hurting others (or perhaps all those who abuse) need to be supported in feeling appropriately guilty. (To clarify: when I say "hurt others," I don't mean yelling at your mother; we're talking severe abuse, like cutting people up with knives. And I'm not talking about *making* people feel guilty, just *letting* them feel guilty.)

I won't take time to list all the ways I was trapped into doing what I did. I just want to say that when I forced my therapist into letting me feel guilty, it was an enormous relief.

It is my guilt, more than anything, that affirms my morality, and that makes me feel different from my parents, who also felt trapped but did not feel guilty. It is wonderful to know how different I am from them.

The weight of my conscience makes me feel secure that I will never do that stuff again. It also drives me to deal with issues about how I have treated my kids as soon as they surfaced. It's no fun to practice abuse prevention, but it's better than living with guilt, and my therapist praises me for how well I am doing it.

I can also accept other people's view of me (people who know nothing about my past) as a good and kind person. That feels wonderful.

Therapists should be completely honest with us no matter how bad it hurts. We have hidden in lies for too many years. Better know who you can touch and who you can't. Always get permission before touching.
—R.C.

Hard-Won Knowledge

By Anne M.

I would like therapists to know that people with MPD must have absolute trust in their therapists more than anything else. I spent a lifetime learning that the people that I loved and trusted could turn and hurt me whenever they pleased. I started always watching others' eyes to read what was going to happen and if I should try to run. My parents trained me not to "tell" anyone or I would be sent away or killed. For a therapist to break trust in any way with a patient with MPD ruins and sets back the whole therapy process.

A therapist who exploits a patient in front of a group, or on video, or even just "testing" teaching techniques for students, commits the ultimate betrayal. After learning to trust the therapist, the walls immediately come back.

What is amazing is that the "host" personality may not realize he or she is being exploited, but some of the others do, and that particular trust, once destroyed, can never be regained.

Please everyone, try to remember that we cannot control the emergence of other personalities. We cannot "fake" the horrible unhappiness this disorder brings. Our emotions, words and actions are very often out of our control. In many cases, we think we are saying one thing and what comes out is very different.

Also, in my own experience, a therapist should answer an MPD's telephone call or request for an additional visit as soon as possible.

It took me so many years to even learn to *ask* for help, that to ask outside of the regularly established parameters meant something very dramatic was happening. It was usually another personality who could not talk in regular session, but who had something important to say. Often the problem concerned extreme depression, fear, or the possibility of suicide.

Please advise patients not to see certain movies (or types of movies) and not to read certain books or stories until you as a professional feel that it won't undo what you have already accomplished. Certain books and movies may trigger memories which the person is not ready to handle.

I certainly don't want to ignore the fact that therapists are people with feelings, bad days, etc. But remember, if you can, to present a calm, untroubled demeanor to a person with MPD. I have learned to be sensitive to people at many different levels. If the therapist is sad, angry, and/or upset, at one of my levels I will see that emotion and think it pertains to me and what I am saying or doing.

If you are unable to cover your feelings, then verbalize to me that you are having this emotion but that in no way does it pertain to me. I am especially afraid of hidden anger and just wait in anticipation for it to explode in verbal or physical assault. Sometimes I wonder if the lump in my throat will ever go away and the heavy "stones" in my stomach will ever be gone.

Setting the Stage for Good Therapy

By Serena

Once treatment begins, we deserve to be told the downside of our diagnosis and therapy, in gentle daily warnings as well as in clear written form.

I have never been able to retrieve my charts, files, and other miscellaneous items, once I have handed them over to the care of therapists. MPD sufferers need to be told not to expect to get original information returned, so they should make copies.

Some set of written precautions or guidelines for treatment boundaries would be helpful.

From the beginning, a financial agreement needs to be clearly stated in writing. A multiple needs to be prepared to sell a car, home, or perhaps even go bankrupt to pay for the treatment. Stated boundaries need to be consistent; giving a client your home phone number and later changing it, is not trust.

Therapists need to have strong moral balance and experience with the stress of family life.

Realistic expectations of the MPD treatment process need to be written individually on a timeline. Here are some statements I would like to hear more often: "It won't always be like this." "I'm sorry this happened to you." "I wish I could have been there with you, let me be there with you now."

I believe that therapists need to model balanced, whole and real-feeling people. They need to be willing to step inside the recesses of an MPD mind and *live* daily the experiences with the client.

MEMO: *Multiple Emergencies*

To: Emergency Medical Technicians/Emergency Room
            Doctors & Nurses
From: A multiple/professional in the medical field
Re: Treatment of patients with Multiple Personality Disorder
            (MPD)

A) Pre-hospital treatment of MPD patient in need of a *psychiatric* evaluation.

1) Introduce yourself.

2) Eliminate unnecessary touching such as taking blood pressure, pulse, checking lung sounds unless medically indicated (i.e., physical injury or overdose).

3) Find out how close the patient will allow you to stand and respect that boundary.

4) Warn the patient before you touch them—even if it is medically warranted.

5) Allow the patient to do as much for self as possible & safe, (i.e., allow patient to step into ambulance, rather than putting on litter; allow patient to ride sitting up; allow patient to buckle him/herself in). See rule #2.

6) Provide privacy (i.e., respect the request for no lights or sirens, close window blinds, don't pry into their psychiatric history).

7) Ask the patient if they need a same sex attendant (EMT) with them.

8) Allow a friend or family member to accompany them in the back of the ambulance. They can be of invaluable assistance.

9) Orient and re-orient the patient as needed.

B) Some things you can expect from an MPD patient when he/she is under stress:

    1) Frequent personality switches:

        —expect changes in how they want to be named

        —expect changes in age (often regression to behavior of young child)

        —expect changes in sex perception (female may say she is a male & vice versa)

        —expect changes in mood/affect

        —expect changes in voice

        —expect changes in academic and/or social functioning level.

    2) Amnesia over past or current events.

    3) Fear of being touched.

C) ER treatment of an MPD patient in need of a *psychiatric* evaluation. First, all of parts *A* & *B* apply!

    1) Allow patient to remain in street clothes. Don't require gowning unless medically necessary for wound examination, self-destructive behavior, etc.

    2) Be aware that normal medical equipment (ie., tourniquet, restraints, enemas, phlebotomy materials) and medical procedures (ie., suturing, gynecological exams) may have been used by the patient's abusers as a part of abuse and therefore, may evoke terror and/or anger.

    3) Allow a friend or family member to stay with the patient in a safe, private area—yet relieve that person of supervisory duties occasionally. (It's stressful.)

    4) Allow patient to move around room (sit on floor, etc.).

    5) Especially with child and/or frightened alters:

        —Be reassuring.

        —Use simple vocabulary and simple sentence construction.

        —Draw if needed.

    In summary: *Be Flexible!*
        Treat Them with Respect!

Abreaction

Kimberly J.

There are no words to express
The feelings that overwhelm me when
Thunderbolts of understanding come.
The shutter snaps,
Locking out the light
And locking me inside.
A vision of another time, another place.
A little girl in lavender and bows,
Ringlets of white curls
On her shoulders,
Lovingly twisted and made to dry.
The lavender gets dirty and the bows fall out
Along with the curls.
Hands are tied, twisted mercilessly.
Tighter and tighter
The blood locked out,
Cold locked in.
All the while a burning heat
Blazes inside
Pleasure and pain combined.
The cold and heat living in one little body
Who can't escape.
No! Don't touch me! she cries.
The shutter snaps
And the burning blaze brightens.
Breath gets shallow and it's oh so heavy.
The weight is so heavy.
Quietly she slips away.
Locked inside
Where no one can reach her coldness,
Her heat.
He doesn't even realize she is not there.
She has gone to where it is warm and dry and dark.

The shutter is closed and she can't see anymore.
No one knows
And no one cares.

Until you.

5

THERAPY
DISAPPOINTMENTS

*Don't just drop a label like MPD on a patient
and walk out the door like you said "It's only the
flu." You'd better have a network of information
for the shocked client, or expect more late-night
crisis calls. —Wendy W.*

An Open Mind. A Closed Therapist.

By Caitlin M.

I was not formally diagnosed with MPD. I came to it on my own, and I
knew that it was right.

At that time, I was seeing a psychiatrist who worked from a fairly
traditional perspective. He often worked with children and had even tes-
tified in court about child abuse. I began to have memories of abuse. The
memories followed one another in orderly fashion, beginning with the
least terrible abuse, such as my father sexually abusing me in the bath
when I was three, and progressing to increasingly painful and degrading
memories involving both of my parents and others.

As each new level of memory came up, I was sure it was the last. How
much more evil could my parents be?

But with this flood of memories there were no alters; I didn't know
I had MPD, and didn't know anything about it. I noted at the time a

curious thing: when the memories came up, I felt myself really in them, reliving them totally as if they were happening right at the time, as if the past were present. Why that was, I didn't know.

It did not occur to my then-therapist to look for MPD, as he knew nothing about it. He became increasingly unable to assimilate the tortures I was describing once I got beyond basic incest. It disturbed him more and more that I couldn't just "talk" about the memories, but needed to scream and relive.

He asked me why I couldn't talk rationally, and I said I didn't know, but that the terror in the memories was real and present and I had to scream.

Finally, one night at home, I was dealing with the first memory of ritual torture—a satanic ritual murder memory. I was out of my mind with terror, reliving the knife, the blood, the chanting, the people in black robes. Suddenly I heard a voice in my mind saying, "My name is Karen, and that happened to me." I sat up in astonishment, wondering if I were losing my mind for real. I had no literature, no supportive therapist, nothing . . . except one thing. I regularly attended an SIA (Survivors of Incest Anonymous) group, and I had just two weeks before heard someone share about MPD. I called her. A small, new group was forming for those with MPD, and I went to the second meeting.

Without that friend, I don't know what I would have done. I thought I was literally crazy because I was hearing voices in my head. I felt suicidal because I didn't want to share "my" life with other inside people, and I felt so foolish and useless and bizarre I thought maybe I should just die. I immediately felt cut off from the normal world. I relied totally on this one friend to give me perspective and help me see that MPD was an appropriate response to childhood hell, and the alters were parts of me who took suffering on my behalf so we could all survive. The new meeting was my only support on the subject for many months. My therapist did not understand MPD, and would not read any literature about it. He spoke to child alters as adults. He kept saying I was using alters to hide from my transference toward him, and he would not follow the paths my system had developed for keeping and guarding feelings.

The more this therapist refused to understand, the more I tried to make him do so, until I was feeling terribly trapped and resentful.

At the group meeting I learned to listen to my child alters. I learned to always protect them and make them feel safe. I learned to go through all my memories and let myself feel or move in whatever way I needed to.

Eventually, after eight more agonizing months, I broke from my "closed" therapist and sought one who understood MPD and ritual torture.

I was able to leave the doubting therapist because, through the meeting, I got my hands on some literature from the Chicago International Society for the Study of Multiple Personality & Dissociation (ISSMP&D) conference, and found myself. When I read articles by Dr. Kluft about MPD, and read about therapists understanding and working with MPD, I didn't feel like such an outcast, and I moved on.

As I look back, I really wish I had started with a therapist who could have been even slightly supportive and understanding about MPD. I had to struggle with it all alone. I knew perfectly well I had it, because I felt completely at home, filled with a deep sense of rightness, as soon as alters were able to speak. But I had to struggle with feelings of being crazy all alone. I paid him to be supportive and help me, and he completely dropped the ball.

I wish too that he'd had clearer vision, and could have suspected I had MPD, and led me to it gently, helping me with the struggles.

One of the things that frustrated me the most was his theory that I didn't "really" have separate alters, but was "using" them to hide from feelings about him. That pseudo-Freudian attitude enraged me. I was grieved more than anything else that he would not believe me, would not follow me in the paths I had. The self-diagnosis and reading on my own and learning everything alone was hell. I wish he had studied it and understood its clinical implications better.

And for myself, I wish I had known that MPD didn't make me crazy; that it was the best possible defense. I wish I had known that there were those who were dealing with it competently, and could offer me hope that I might have a functional, integrated personality someday. For although my MPD is smooth, and I don't lose time or do dreadful self-mutilations, I want to integrate when the time comes. I had no support for knowing, I had to learn it all myself. I wish I had known that traumatic flashbacks were common, that hallucinations about time and reality were common, that all alters are part of my life equally. I wish I had had a professional to talk to about my fears. I thought then that perhaps I was incurable. I did most definitely not feel that I belonged in the "normal" world.

Abuse in Therapy

By Julie W.

To The Therapists: Having spent three and one-third of the last four years with an abusive therapist (psychiatrist) who seemed to think he was God, got a vicarious thrill out of my childhood, and occasionally enjoyed putting his thrills into action, I'm pretty opinionated. Here's what I want *all* therapists to know:

1) **Keep your hands to yourself.** Child alters are in an adult body and that body has no business in your lap, being kissed, being cuddled. It is not your place to "teach" us the pleasures of physical contact.

2) **You're not our parents.** We don't need to be calling you "Daddy." You can't replace what never was and never will be. Child alters are not "your children" and you cannot re-raise us.

3) **Keep your opinions and emotions to yourself.** We don't need your tears or your anger. We have a gracious plenty of our own. We don't need you to criticize our abusers, we can do just fine ourselves. We don't need you to cry over us or with us. We need your strength, acceptance and understanding, not your pity or anger.

4) **Don't foster and encourage our dependence, helplessness and fears.** We can't learn independence, strength and courage if you present yourself as omnipotent or attempt to guide our every thought. Playing God may be fun, and for us, having someone who will love and protect us at every turn is enticing and seductive, but *you're not God and we're not children!*

5) **We're not there for your entertainment.** Things that happened are not substance for "let's amaze the neighbors." Don't tell or hint at our stories to others (especially to those who know us), other multiples included. As patients, we have our own demons, we don't need each other's. If you think the gory details of cruelty are exciting, you're in a lot worse shape than we are.

6) **I'm not your therapist.** All the MPDs I know are good talkers and magnificent listeners. But we don't need to hear your marital/financial/parenting/professional problems. Take the money we pay you and go get your own therapist.

7) **You are not going to heal us.** Given support, guidance, boundaries, the freedom to err, make our own decisions, patience, honesty, we

are the only ones who can heal us. *You are not a mechanic, and we are not cars.*

8) **Remember that we are real, living, breathing people**. At the end of the hour, we don't get to leave our memories behind. You don't need to hear all the details before you start dealing with the emotions. If you separate the events and the emotions, you are compounding and reinforcing the MPD existence.

Dubious Treatment

By Ken M.

Looking back, I wish I had known about the biological-medicalism of some psychiatrists and their disregard of ethics.

My MPD clinician diagnosed me MPD and later admitted me to a psychiatric hospital. Unknown to her and me until later, the psychiatrist in charge resisted the diagnosis of MPD. After a thorough round of testing indicated no epilepsy, the psychiatrist said, "I *still* know you're an epileptic."

Meanwhile, he continued medication consisting of 900 mg of Tegretol (for "hallucinations") and 400 mg of Desipramine daily. The latter was over the therapeutic limit; I could have had a heart attack. Also, it fed my lifetime eating disorder; I ballooned up to 280 pounds.

In retrospect, I realize that the psychiatrist and his intern intended to break my relationship with my MPD clinician. I started hearing plans for "integrating" me with Tegretol and sending me to an incest group for men. Meanwhile, behind her back, these two "professionals" told me their shop talk about her—for example, their discussions over dinner at an international psychiatric conference attended by the hospital psychiatrists.

Then the intern told me a devastating "secret" about my therapist. (It was a lie—but some of my sexually-abused teen male alters believed it because they had still to work through transference.)

My therapy stopped. Fortunately my MPD clinician noticed, confronted me, and I revealed the "secret." She then confronted the two psychiatrists. My psychiatrist (who was also medical director) apologized. His intern never did. I was discharged. This episode cost me and my therapist many months of work to rebuild trust.

During my second hospitalization at another facility, on a Dissociative Disorders unit, I learned from my new psychiatrist just how devastating the abuse by the two previous psychiatrists had been. My new psychiatrist was overwhelmed by the details; he suggested I seek legal assistance.

It took months to think through this trauma by the doctors. Finally, I realized that a lawsuit would be counter-productive; details of my incest and multiplicity would be made public; it would cost both myself and my therapist years. I decided against suing.

Fortunately, I learned to trust my new psychiatrist; he accepted MPD and he facilitated rebuilding trust with my therapist. On the Dissociative Disorders unit I made rapid progress. My therapist helped me abreact my alters' trauma. Very shortly afterwards she helped me to integrate.

I wish I knew then what I know now: it could have saved two years of additional trauma—trauma at the hands of biological-medical psychiatrists who have no ethics. Ironically, both still practice and are "respected professionals."

While struggling to make sure the diagnosis of MPD adheres to standard scientific and clinical principles so that they can establish credibility for themselves, their research, and MPD in general, therapists may be losing sight of the subjective experience of what is "real" for the patient.

After several years of my personal work, I have learned that the essence of what I remember is accurate although there may be discordance in the details.

When I read current research articles and books by the "tops" in the field, I'm afraid that they are going to get lost in trying to verify abuse which can't always be verified, and in maintaining a therapeutically neutral position for the sake of a pure transference relationship.

Remember you are sitting with a human being. Please be professional but also please be authentic with us. —Alice O.

Born Too Soon?

By Lucia C.

What I want to say most to therapists is really a plea—a plea for compassion or maybe just the withholding of judgment.

I am a forty-three year old woman who has finally been given hope after so many years of enduring, sometimes owning, but thank God never quite accepting the negative judgments, the blaming and damning rejection of those "helpers" from whom I sought release from my internal hell.

I never really understood why I was constantly accused of lying when I worked so hard to be honest, of being manipulative when base survival was my aim. Since some of my alters had long accepted that they were unredeemably evil and some thought that we weren't supposed to be in this world in the first place, the more outside evidence there was from authority figures that what those parts believed was true the harder it was for those determined to survive to do so.

Then there were the alters who saw the betrayal, the total lack of fairness in the world. The anger that was already present from my childhood horror was compounded. Each abusive person, each injustice was a hand turning up the thermostat on a boiler with a defective safety valve.

How many times I wanted to be as crazy as some said I was or as evil and conscienceless as others implied!

I didn't know why I was so uncontrollable . . . why people would say I was childish . . . why there was an angry one who swore like a sailor and would lose me friends and get me in trouble with people who needed to see me as a nice person.

I didn't know why were there sainted parts who would make promises that others had no intention of keeping . . . or the shy parts . . . and those parts who were politically committed, sometimes strongly on opposite sides of an ideal.

The arguments inside my head were enormous. People who would know one part would not even recognize or believe the other parts. They would say one part or the other was play-acting—especially when encountering the self-destructive parts.

There was always one who would desperately go for help to keep another (inside) from killing us. But nobody ever saw there was more than one person in me, so disbelief would follow. This caused us to use somewhat manipulative measures to stay alive.

Those of us whose life began with an unrelieved abusive childhood are bound to have trouble learning to form a trusting relationship with anyone. But I (and others like me) have so many years post-childhood damage to sift through before I can even trust my therapist enough to have a *normal* lack of trust. It is frustrating, excruciating work. I hope she has the patience for it.

Maybe I was born too early. Maybe it wasn't anyone's fault that MPD wasn't recognized. The whole idea frightens people. It frightens me!

But I didn't deserve the childhood that formed me and I didn't deserve the kind of pain I received in the name of help.

So my plea is this: If you come across a client/patient you don't understand, don't dismiss them and close your mind, or hide your lack of knowledge with recriminations. Try opening to new possibilities. You might find a miracle of creative human survival called Multiple Personality.

Guinea Pig? Teaching Tool? It's Not "Therapy" for Me!

By D.L.I.

When I received your call for submissions to this publication, " . . . *an educational tool for therapists and family members* . . . " my first response was to throw the darned thing out! My hostility and frustration stem from being repeatedly used as a guinea pig for "fascinated" and "curious" onlookers, as though the manifestations of my acute pain (the various personalities) were some sort of wild and glorious transcendent paranormal experience.

In some instances other people envied my MPD as a talent, as if I dreamed up other "suave characters" to do my dirty work or to titillate an audience. (The "darker" personalities were feared or ignored.)

In this I became objectified, a form of dehumanization. My pain was laughed at when a "cute" child alter emerged. Often, an important message of an alter got totally ignored if that alter's behavior didn't meet with another person's approval or expectations.

My attempts to recreate and thereby resolve past trauma were considered a most dramatic form of entertainment—especially for hospital staff and a few "friends" who used my neediness and vulnerability to their own advantage. (Hospital staff, incidentally, includes residents, interns, and nursing students doing a rotation through the psychiatric unit.)

The real issues of severe child abuse, sexual molestation, deprivation, and the long sad story of a lost childhood were completely misplaced among the requests for impromptu switches. My confidentiality and privacy were often violated in favor of some new person wanting to hear jokes from a sexy adolescent personality.

But the worst came at school when a teacher announced that there was an interesting case of MPD pinned to a bulletin board announcing the latest psychology issues. Interested myself, I looked at the article syndicated from a remote town in California (I live on the East Coast) where my therapist had given a lecture about MPD to an audience of other professionals. There I found a complete description of my entire system!

I was subsequently subjected to hearing the comments of my classmates and teacher when the class resumed.

As I look back on those experiences I realize now, with a moderate level of forgiveness, that few of the people who used me did it with intentional harm in mind . . . though, harm it did! I felt a deep sense of betrayal. Each time someone asked me to "perform" for them I had a sense that my needs were being subjugated to someone else's, a common situation in my past. When such requests came from a professional I not only forfeited opportunities to build trust and learn about safe relationships, but the pattern of role reversal, so common in families that produce MPD patients, was reinforced.

Each time I was asked, inappropriately, to identify "which one I was," my privacy was intruded upon and the relational boundaries, again, were up-ended (especially in situations where a professional was involved).

While a professional may need to know which alter is present, it is equally important to respect the client's need for safety. In most cases, MPDs have carefully hidden alter identities (even from themselves) in order to cope with the shame of "losing time" as well as the intolerable trauma which originated the other personalities. These patterns die hard when they represent a lifetime of coping.

It is essential for therapists of all sorts to exercise utmost sensitivity when asking who an alter is and what they represent. But even more important is the atmosphere in which MPDs are treated. It should be repeatedly emphasized that personalities are not for the fun and amusement of staff and others but represent a serious ongoing attempt to "tell the story,"—an unspeakable story that was so terrible it takes many voices to tell.

Before beginning intensive therapy with a diagnosis of Dissociative Disorder-Not Otherwise Specified, I was warned that the treatment I had chosen would be lengthy and arduous.

That didn't faze me. I was a survivor and highly motivated. Three years have passed. I am just beginning to realize that my chances of succeeding at this are remote.

Everything I read in journals and publications concerned with dissociation seems to concentrate on favorable outcomes. In spite of trying hard, I am not a success at changing.

Psychotherapy has brought about considerable gains for which I am most grateful, but I haven't achieved the primary objective which was the focus of my therapy. I'm disappointed with myself and wonder if there are others like me.

At my request my therapy has been terminated. —Jeannine N.

A Lengthy Search for Treatment

By Ann H.

I'm grateful for this chance to vent my frustrations over my long search for appropriate treatment.

I'm forty-five years old. I've seen over forty therapists, some for one session, some for months, since I was in college. For the last three years I've finally had very effective intensive psychotherapy; I've made significant changes so I'm in a lot less physical and emotional pain, and am far more functional. Prozac put a "floor" under my severe depression, making therapy more effective as well.

At one time I had fifty distinct personalities. Although we're not intentionally doing fusions, my alters soften their boundaries naturally as we deal with our feelings. Here is some of what this process has taught me:

1. *MPD is not all bad.* The various "people" give quick, direct access to the issues which other patients may have to struggle to achieve.

2. *The results of child abuse are far, far worse than I imagined.* I have always felt damaged, different, insecure, and badly hurt by my childhood. A lot more can be corrected than I ever thought possible, though.

3. *Society should pay more attention to emotional child abuse and emotional incest (which did a lot of the damage to me).* I've had this abuse discounted by several therapists, some of whom hadn't dealt with being abused themselves. Actually, I think these types of abuse are harder to identify and treat because they're less obvious.

4. *How the therapist deals with his own feelings and needs, rather than any technique, is the biggest determiner of whether the therapy will work and how well the patient will get.* It is hard to be more honest with your feelings than your therapist is willing to be with his.

My feelings are very intense. It is amazing the number of ways therapists have found to avoid dealing with feelings, to make me wrong for not getting well faster, or to punish me because they did not want to hear something, even though I was not being abusive. I've had them shorten sessions, spend a lot of time on light conversation when I made it clear I was there for therapy, tell inappropriate, tantalizing tidbits about other patients, hold sessions at midnight or later on a routine basis (in the hospital), threaten to see me even less when I complained about late sessions, try to focus on problem solving (which I generally do very well on my own), blame me for problems I acknowledge, am working on, and already feel very bad about.

One of the things I hate the most is therapists or staff saying something is "for your own good" when it is clearly for them and they won't acknowledge it. Hospital staff often interfered with therapy by trying to get me not to cry, and in other ways dumping their problems on me.

5. *MPD patients are not all the same.* I got sick of having techniques crammed down my throat because "they work on MPD." For example, my host personality was obsessive-compulsive and needed to be treated as such, not as some generic "borderline" or "histrionic" that some theory says applies to all MPDs.

6. *Visualization is not possible for everyone, or, techniques have (usually unstated) contexts and prerequisites necessary to make them work.* My child personalities need concrete, kinesthetic experiences instead of adult talk and visualizations.

For instance, I was so terrorized that it took months of experiencing safety in a hospital to build up meaning for the word "safe." Also, there was so much craziness in my family that I had to make continual conscious efforts to remain sane; I've felt I'll literally lose my hold on reality if I give visualizations enough reality to make them work.

149

7. *Visualization is not the answer to everything.* Feelings are literally trapped in my body, held in by muscle tension. If I am going to get truly well, and not just learn a few more coping devices, I must really have these feelings in order to let go of them. As I've released feelings with the support of my therapist, the enormous amount of muscle tension in my body has decreased, and physical symptoms have improved without ever having to directly work on them.

8. *How damaged a person is by abuse depends upon the resources they had as well as the nature of the traumas.* The amount of isolation I created made the abuse far more damaging. Many therapists couldn't see what the deprivation had done to me, making me feel worse.

9. *Only as my needs have been met, have I gotten better.* Some therapists have actually said that it was good for me not to have a session, no matter what I thought, because it would teach me not to be so needy. Then I guess all I need to get well is to drop therapy entirely!

Others seem to treat MPDs as if they have undamaged adults who can take over; both my adults and my children are severely damaged, and the damage hurts excruciatingly.

10. *Meeting my needs has required a lot of what could be called "reparenting" by my therapist.* I cannot understand how some experts can say that this isn't necessary. How my therapist treats me and the relationship is what heals me, not some technique.

I do not need or want someone to be an "architect" for me to consult. I constantly do therapeutic work on my own, and I'm not stupid. I don't want someone off safe in the distance, in their mind, and not emotionally very present.

Another misconception (this one held particularly by hospital staff), is that concrete activities like holding someone are "beneath" them, and not what they're paid to do. What my kids need is real help and a real relationship. I've had profound, organic changes in my thinking due to this reparenting. (And I haven't bothered my therapist with incessant phone calls, etc.)

11. *I wish many of my therapists had gotten effective help to deal with their own feelings and my MPD.* Why do so many feel they must "wing-it" for months on end while they collect their fees, the therapy flounders, and I'm in pain? I *can* tell they don't know what they're doing and it creates panic. Poor therapy has created more traumas for me to work out later. It seems only ethical to get *effective* help when needed. (And I do mean

effective help, not just a token case conference with others who know no more than you do.)

12. *Please listen.* I'm sick of prior therapists not listening and dismissing everything I say as some form of resistance. This is crazy-making, disrespectful, and not therapeutic.

We have experienced a lot of hurt. Now we are numb. We do not experience pain or understand feelings beyond frustration. Stop insinuating that "we don't like you, or that you are making us angry." We do not know "anger," as you seem to refer to it. —Anonymous

I'd like my therapist to understand that I don't find relief in the diagnosis of MPD. I don't have control over the ability to dissociate. My alters don't want to be in therapy and I can't always communicate what I hear inside. When I call my therapist, it is because I want to die, I have already tried to deal with it and couldn't. Sometimes I just want to know that he is there and don't really want him to do anything. I don't like him to dig too much because when I leave I am alone with the information for at least a week.

I wish he would dig at the beginning of the session so I can deal with it. I would like a ten-minute warning that the session is nearly over. When he walks out after fifty minutes, I feel rejected and leave angry. —Anne C.

Inner Wisdom

By J. Robert

The host may attempt to present her/himself as a competent individual who has control over her/his alternates and/or destiny. Do not be misled by this charade. We, as alternates, would not exist if the host were truly in control at any given moment.

If our host is characteristic of MPD, you will find your client to be either guilt or anxiety-ridden, prone to shame, reticent with regards to self-disclosure, and/or greatly disoriented at any given time—even more so following loss of time.

Time is a four-letter-word to our host. It is a gift that can be stolen at a moment's notice and may not be returned for minutes, months, or (what may seem like) a millennia. Whenever possible, provide as detailed an account as is possible for the host with regards to what her/his alternates have said or done during her/his lost time (provided that you have the alternate's permission).

This is as important (if not more so) to the multiple as it is to an individual who has experienced a fever-induced delirium and wishes to know what she/he has done in her/his amnesiac state. Through these detailed accounts, the host can then become more familiar with her/his alternate states and prepare to welcome them to her/his own realm.

It has been my experience (through witnessing over eight years of therapy) that many practitioners in the psychotherapeutic field are loath to address alternates as authentic individuals. We are people too. We have our own values, attitudes, logic and codes of conduct. We, too, are deserving of recognition. To paraphrase a document that many in your nation hold in esteem, "We were molded in the likeness of our Creator and We have been deemed good."

Do not simply humor us. Treat us as you would a significant other, for that is what and who we are: *significant* others.

Lessons Learned From a Failed Therapy

By Nancy G.

My therapist allowed events in her personal life and insecurities in her own personality to affect the therapy. The natural transference process became a massive countertransference. Because our whole life had depended upon reading the signals that others around us gave off (as a protective device), we might have known our therapist better than she knew herself.

She was unable to honestly admit to herself what effect the memories had on her. Slowly, a sort of role reversal began to take place and we ended up "taking care of her" and she, therefore, became another horror from our past. As a result, the therapy which had begun with such promise and hope soon became part of our never ending nightmare and she became one of the leading characters in it.

While the therapist tried to "kid herself" into thinking things were going well, we knew that the therapy was getting progressively worse. In the end, she called in another therapist to assist her, but the wounds on both sides were so deep that the damage was irreparable.

I think that is why this book is so important. Those of us, client and therapist alike, who undertook this therapeutic challenge had so little knowledge of what a difficult and odious journey it would be!

Looking back, we have identified several important points that might have improved our situation:

(1) A therapist must not allow his/her personal life to continually spill over into therapy.

(2) The therapist should honestly admit her own "failings" and then, as much as possible, correct the problems.

(3) Therapists should recognize when they may need to turn to outside sources of help, rather than trying to be a hero who pretends to know all the answers. (Let's face it, none of us do.)

(4) Since we (with MPD) are experts in reading the slightest nuances of problems in therapy or changes in therapy, it's important for the therapist not to pretend that everything is ok or try to cover things up. Such pretense opens up a whole world of misinterpretations.

(5) MPD therapy takes a tremendous amount of commitment on both sides. If either party is unwilling to stick with the commitments, then disaster can result.

(6) The therapist should be able to deal appropriately with hurt and anger.

(7) It's important for therapists to work well with all the different personalities and to not shut themselves off from the client because they can't tolerate certain personalities/abuses that occurred.

(8) Most of all, therapists should not overextend themselves and take on more than they can physically or emotionally handle.

Ten years ago, we started on the journey of healing. In three and a half years, we went through five therapists. Not one of them took the time to find out what the problem was. Three of them wrote prescriptions after we told them we were a drug addict. One of them pushed too hard and when we couldn't answer his questions, told us we didn't want to get better. The last one told us we were hopeless and that we would probably

end up institutionalized for the rest of our life, or die from a suicide attempt. Two years later, we ended up with a therapist who listened, cared, and took the time to find out what was wrong. We are very grateful to her for all she has been through with us and all she has given us.
—Annette K.

HOPE

Normal people can't fully appreciate how wonderful love is and how precious is the relationship with a person who is actually worthy of trust.
—*Jessica Turner*

Why have we made it this far, living through all the atrocities of our childhoods, just to give up on life as adults? The threat of further abuse is finally removed! We *survived* our personal holocaust! We deserve hope, healing, health, and some measure of happiness.

We are not weirdos. We are probably some of the most interesting, creative, talented people you'll ever know. We deserve respect and self-esteem.

We don't want to be gossiped about or ridiculed or made to feel odd.

It is important to know there are still those who will stand by us for the long haul and offer support. I have been blessed to have a therapist and a small circle of friends who know about the struggles of an incest survivor with MPD. When the walls feel as though they are closing in on me or I'm afraid of what I do not know, then I can pick up the phone and someone who understands will be there on the other end. And with or without MPD, we all need friends like that. —Vickie G.

I wish I'd known:
That MPD can be fun.
That each alter has to heal on his/her own.

How upsetting it would be to have a female alter and how educational it would be.
How good it feels to be loved by your others, especially when you can't love yourself.
How much fun the kids can have.
That I'd get closer to my "outside" children.
That having MPD doesn't mean you're crazy.
How prevalent MPD is.
What books to read—and where to find them.
That almost all MPDs are incest victims.
—Charlie Anderson

I wish I'd known that we aren't bad because of what happened to us or because the alters exist. We don't need to be ashamed of the alters.
—By MaryLou P.

I wish I'd known early in MPD therapy the importance of leaving the abusive situation I was living in. Living in a situation where I was not only abused, but literally had to fight for my life, left me with a clouded sense of reality. I was not able to talk to my therapist about things that continuously went on in my living situation because it was all a "secret."

I thought that if I told my therapist what was really going on, he would not believe me; if he did happen to believe me, I was going to be "in big trouble."

I wish I had realized how much living in that awful situation hurt me, mentally as well as physically. I felt that I had no one I could trust, not even my therapist.

Most importantly, I realized that the abuse only perpetuated the disorder. Instead of getting better I got worse.

I finally reached a point where I could go no further, I *had* to get out, and I did. Unfortunately, I also had to leave a therapist that I had worked with for years because I had to run away from home at the age of twenty-five.

Since I left home my life has improved remarkably. I no longer concentrate on surviving from one day to the next; I have a plan and goals in my life. Greatest of all, I no longer seek to get better, I long to be WELL.
—Eunice S.

The Survival Factors

By ME

I would have liked a list of symptoms typical of MPD soon after my diagnosis. I would have liked to have gone through the list with my therapist; to have had the opportunity to claim and explain the symptoms and/or behaviors I recognized within myself. It would have been helpful to me for my therapist to explain her observations about me as we worked our way through the list. She did this informally over a long period of time, so I didn't get a clear understanding for a while.

My therapist educated me, so by the time we decided I had MPD, I knew a lot. The knowledge that was helpful is as follows:

—I am very intelligent or I would not have been able to develop this alternative way of adapting to my environment, which allowed me to function.

—I developed these closed-off, secret, compartmentalized parts of me for the purpose of saving my own life. The kind of abuse that causes dissociative multiplicity, is life threatening.

—I did not split off to get out of anything or to get away with anything. I did it to preserve my own life. I split off out of sheer necessity and not out of desire. My multiplicity was about functioning and surviving extremely severe circumstances. The fact that I needed to split off is not my fault or responsibility.

—Although I have been deeply depressed and suicidal most of my life I have a very strong core self, with a great desire not only to survive, but to thrive. I have MPD because I want to live.

—I am not weak or stupid. I am strong and have an unusual capacity to cope with pain.

—Having MPD proves that I have tremendous potential and ability to change because I have demonstrated this ability throughout my life. I am making the necessary changes to get well.

—Although the MPD I have created feels like a monster at times (now no longer effective or functional in my life) I have within me the drive, tools and ability to do whatever is necessary to achieve complete recovery.

—The purpose of my therapy is to be responsible for my own recovery, knowing that professionals will guide, encourage, listen, and accept me on my journey to integrated, mature, adult functioning.

157

—I am in charge and have within me all the tools I need to control my identities claiming responsibility, ownership, and behavior of all parts of myself. I will do my work towards integration at my own pace.

There are also benefits to being multiple that we weren't aware of. Multiplicity is not only a creative way to survive, it can also be a creative way to recover. We have a built-in support system that is there at 4:00 in the morning and we don't have to wait for them to wake up.

There is always someone around to play with or to talk to. Since we have a wide range of interests and capabilities, we can have a wide range of friends. We do not have to be restricted by a single frame of reference.

Most importantly, we wish we had known that all people are not going to see us as flawed or crippled. Some people will honor our survival.

When I was first told about the diagnosis of MPD, I was relieved because it explained so many things from the past that made me feel crazy, insane or just acting out for attention. We had spent forty years trying to understand why we were so different, now we knew. Almost simultaneously, we found out that our twin sister, younger sister and eldest brother had the same diagnosis, which explained a lot of the *normalcy* we thought existed as we were growing up. —Peggy J.

I was first given the diagnosis of MPD four years ago when I asked my therapist if I was manic depressive. When she told me that my diagnosis was MPD I was actually relieved. I had taken psychology courses and knew enough about Manic Depressive Illness to be afraid.

MPD was a different story. When I decided to go out and find information, I found that very little existed. It was very frustrating. My therapist gave me articles from a journal on Dissociative Disorders. They were informative but led to more questions. I've been trying to think of things that I wish that I had known when I was first diagnosed. For each thing that I wish I'd known then, I now realize that it was too soon. It is just as important not to have too much information as it is not to have too little. It was difficult to accept the fact that I am multiple and very easy to fall back on the wish that I was making it all up.

I wish that I had known from the beginning that other multiples experience such strong denial of the multiplicity and abuse in their lives.

Even after four years of living with the diagnosis there are still questions. I recently read *Treatment and Diagnosis of Multiple Personality Disorder* by Frank Putnam, M.D. I found it to be very helpful. I learned one thing in particular from this book that I wish I had known early on. He mentions that deception in MPD is usually part of the coping mechanism and not (in my words) an expression of "badness."

Although I love and respect my therapist, I have deceived her many times. I have suffered a lot of guilt for those deceptions. It was very helpful to be told that this is not an indication that I'm a "bad" person.

I realize today that the things I wanted to know at the beginning of treatment might have caused me to run from therapy, if I had actually known them. If I had realized the extent of abuse associated with the onset of MPD or the length of treatment time, I think that I would have crumpled in despair. I am grateful to my therapist for giving me the information that I needed only as I asked for it or for which her intuition/experience told her it was time. —Susan B.

I wish I'd known techniques early on (such as tape recorders, bulletin boards and journals/videos) to facilitate getting to know and accept my alters.

I wish I'd known my alters are strong parts of me. They were originally created as protectors, not enemies. They do not mean to hurt me. —Kim B.

The End of Innocence

By Dorothy P.

Looking back at my therapy, I wonder whether it would have helped had I recognized at the outset that acceptance of the diagnosis and commencement of therapy represented the end of innocence and the beginning of responsibility. Most people think innocence was lost long before therapy began, and I don't disagree, especially in cases of physical abuse.

There are other kinds of innocence, one kind being the innocence we maintain by remaining helpless. While we are instinctively aware that our lives are painful and sometimes even destructive, we are afraid and either don't know how or sincerely believe we can't change. We remain helpless and our helplessness becomes a defense.

I know because that was me. I blindly hid, the victim of childish fears and beliefs that controlled my life, and I was helpless to do anything about it.

Slowly and reluctantly I learned that no one can do my work for me. Like it or not, I am responsible for consoling my childish parts and moving on.

It is hard to explain how it feels to accept that responsibility: sadness at the loss of an old, familiar crutch; pride in knowing I can take care of myself; confidence in the knowledge that the victimization can't happen again.

My therapist would surely wonder if she knew this had been written by the little girl who sat sniffling on her couch last week. Accepting responsibility for my own healing isn't easy. It is a long, hard, up and down process. Running away and hiding behind my helplessness would be so much easier than staying in therapy. It is a struggle every day. But I have truly come to believe that we each must make the transition from innocence to responsibility if we are to heal and grow to maturity.

It was extremely important for us that we have discipline, consistency, and structure. We were so out of control. The small ones were overlooked by the older ones. The aggressive terrorized the weak, and we were always stepping all over each other.

We needed to respect each other. We needed to cooperate so that the time lapses were fewer.

In the past, there had been many self-abuse episodes, as well as suicide attempts and attacks on each other. When we found our doctor, we became aware of cooperation and how it works.

He is very rigid about our giving 100% effort, signing contracts against abuse (mental or physical), and for honesty. He has opened up a new world to us and we realize how much we do care about each other (although we still get on each others' nerves a lot of the time).

Finally, we're learning to create a common front against an abusive past as we move toward a healthier future. —Kathy A.

For me, having someone understand the constant turmoil, confusion, and indecision in my head was a tremendous relief.

I had always debated every decision with myself all of my life. I assumed that everyone experienced this and simply handled it better than I.

When my therapist and I began to "talk with" and explore these other "opinions" and identify their origins, my self-esteem immediately began to improve and the circle began to be positive instead of negative.

To be assured by a professional that you were indeed dealing with factors that not everyone has to deal with is very comforting.

I also think that it is important for the therapist to believe what he hears while maintaining a sense of reality. —Lillian F.

Please remember that this pain we suffer is the pain of growth. I fought through it to the other side. I am alive with hope. I get better and better at processing the despair that I often feel as a result of the reorganization of my self. I bite off large chunks of growth matter. I am ok. And I will be ok. I am learning to trust myself, and my ability to process life. Life is better and better for it. To know that the quality of life depends solely on your self and the choices you make, is at once crushing and freeing. —Margaret O.

I am becoming free.
free to love
free to laugh
free to be mad
free to be glad
free to be me
—just watch . . .
you'll see.
Life is a dance. The neat thing about dances is . . . they can change. Back and forth—always evolving. —Margaret O.

I lost my childhood to abuse; creating multiple personalities saved my life.

I lost a lot of developmental steps into my thirties because I was so split. I lost a lot of just plain living during five years of treatment.

But now, I am no longer a victim. My treatment is my choice so that I don't lose any more life, my life. My goal is to thrive, not just survive.

I believe I will achieve this because I believe in myself for the first time in my whole life. —Alice O.

Gifted Responses

By Margaret O.

I have become very appreciative of my multiplicity. I enjoy my many facets. Being in touch with so much of myself brings into life a rich vibrancy.

It is not, however, without its complications. The way I process seems different than other people. I believe it is a very fine process but it does require that I teach those around me how it functions and how they can best respond to it.

Now that I am a recovering MPD, fully integrated and functioning well, it is important that those around me understand the time factor involved in my processing of information, feelings, etc.

My first reaction is not necessarily my total reaction. Especially with important issues, I tend to go through a check-off of reactions (feelings). My friends and family know to wait until all reactions have surfaced. This takes time but the end result is an honest assessment of what the situation is, how I feel about it, and what my needs are. Then I am acting—not reacting. On some occasions I have conflicting and contradictory responses to the same event. It is hard to know which is primary when both cannot be accommodated.

I do not have a solution, other than to wait, because time will often allow an unconscious sifting and sorting that may bring resolution.

Another thing my intimate others know about me is that I need lots of space, alone time, solitude. I am not a superficial thinker. I need the time and space to process creatively and spontaneously. This is how I regenerate.

However, I also need lots of interpersonal analysis, talk, and sharing time with others. It is not always easy to find people who like to do that.

In the stages of full-blown MPD, the above holds true at an even more intense level. People found it helpful to know what I learned about MPD, that it was a gifted response to a traumatic situation. They learned to trust their instincts, and not to take it personally if, for example, I became abusive. They learned not to be afraid of the selves, to face them directly with compassion, sensitivity, honesty, and sincerity. It helped those closest to me to read *Guiding The Gifted Child* and *The Drama of The Gifted Child*, by Alice Miller.

I had to teach them what my needs were as I learned what they were.

It was especially helpful that I had lots of assurance from my brother and his family that they would not abandon me, not just physically but in their belief in me. I needed to feel that they perceived me as sane, not crazy. I was all there. I just had to blend it all together in a way that worked for me.

It helped that I had others who had absolute faith in me.

A Different View of Me

By Marita B.

When I started with my therapist, I thought a lot differently about myself than I do today. I had no real feelings such as sadness or happiness. I thought my feelings weren't worth having, and I had spent my life stuffing them.

I couldn't remember things in my past . . . my childhood . . . my marriage. I didn't know why I was like this.

I thought love meant pain. I thought everything that happened to me was my fault, because I was never good enough.

In our early sessions, I spent time in mind games, trying to keep things to myself. I was scared that I would be abandoned by my therapist. I didn't trust her. I spent much time rebelling against the diagnosis, remembering, and being withdrawn.

I was so scared of telling my story to her. I really thought she would stop seeing me as a person, and instead reflect my negative feelings about myself.

At the end of our session, she got up and hugged me. She told me she was still there. I didn't blow her away.

From that day forward, I learned to trust her. I knew she wasn't going to be condescending. She was going to see me as the unique individual I am, not as a textbook case.

It is still hard to be open with her today. I am starting to catch myself when I do this. If I can't tell her out loud, I write letters to her. I don't play mind games.

When I am self-destructive or suicidal, she doesn't panic. She listens to me and gives me feedback for alternatives.

She has taught me I can have feelings and express them to her. If I get angry at her, she doesn't push me away. She pulls me closer to her, by accepting me as me.

My therapist makes me see my problems in the real world as they are. She doesn't let me off easy . . . not at all. In fact, she has taught me I don't live in a Black & White World, that life isn't an either/or situation.

I no longer take on the responsibilities of other people. I am only responsible for my own feelings. I can change me—no one else. We have come a long way.

She is supportive of me making my own decisions, using my judgment, whether she likes it or not. She tells me how she feels about it, but she is flexible, no hard and fast rules for situations. She recognizes things are hard for me to cope with.

My therapist already knows what helps me; I don't want her to change. I need her just to be herself. When I met her it was like doors opening up for me. It was like love pouring in.

We Weave the Cloth of Healing

By L.P.

It has been my experience that there were not one, but three crucial factors at play in my initial work toward acceptance of the multiplicity after initial diagnosis. All three were interwoven, and alternately pulled against or meshed with each other, working to either destroy the fabric of acceptance or to weave themselves together to create a beautiful design. These three factors were:

1. the attitude of the therapist.

2. the information I was given concerning multiplicity.

3. the information I desperately wanted, but was unavailable at the time.

I feel that the manner in which my therapist handled the initial disclosure of the diagnosis and ensuing information on MPD was crucial to my rapid progress.

Her gentle approach and openness engendered an open, trusting, cooperative attitude on my part. If handled differently, such information could have pushed me even further into the fearful isolation in which I was burying myself.

To me, the manner of imparting information is as important as the information itself.

My therapist did the following, all of which were extremely valuable:

1. She constantly allayed my fears that I was crazy, pointing out that it was the alters that *kept me from going crazy.*

2. She continuously validated me as a special individual with talents and abilities that enabled me to make a contribution to this world.

3. She frequently pointed out (after all the work I already had done on the abuse issues), that diagnosis would not necessarily double the time I must remain in treatment, but that it was a major breakthrough which would enable me to proceed much more quickly through treatment.

4. She emphasized that multiplicity is a very effective coping skill given to a child to enable her to endure untold horrors and still be able to remain in life's mainstream.

5. She pointed out that multiples can be, in fact, highly gifted, especially in creative pursuits. It's been my experience, in fact, that the innate capacity for creativity with which each person is born is often suppressed through our culture's efforts to make a child conform. In multiples, however, that creative potential is walled off and preserved by alters, being allowed to express itself from time to time without the host personality's awareness that anything out of the ordinary is happening. When that creative personality is tapped, however, the potential is astounding.

6. She gave me information on the capacity of multiples to be in direct contact with their Centers (the guiding Spirit within, the link with the Higher Power.) This prompted my Center to reveal herself. Since that time, my Center, in her wisdom, has guided my therapists and me through a rapid succession of the worst of the memories heretofore unavailable and through an amazing journey into the world of the Spirit.

Constantly at play against those factors was an intense need to read all I could concerning multiplicity, but at that point there were no more than four books, all autobiographies, available for a layperson to read. I felt like an alien dropped from the sky on a strange planet with no road map or directions to point where I should go. I hungered for a *Courage to Heal* for multiples—a book which would:

1. explain the disorder in lay terms.

2. share experiences of other MPDs so I wouldn't feel so alone.

3. give me a set of projected steps I could expect to follow through treatment, ever knowing they would be tentative at best.

4. outline methods to help deal with the disruption caused by the alters.

Steps 1, 3, and 4 have since been addressed by the therapists as they've come up, but I wanted the comfort of *immediate* information upon diagnosis.

The experience of multiplicity, while at times disconcerting, has been an indescribably valuable gift to me.

I am a victim of extreme sexual, physical, and emotional abuse which commenced around the age of three. The sexual and physical abuse ceased around age sixteen or seventeen and the emotional abuse is still attempted to this day.

In spite of the horrendous acts perpetrated against me as a child, and most of all thanks to the alters, I was miraculously able to be a straight-A student in grade school and middle school and an honor student in high school, winning numerous academic and social awards. This was all the work of the alters. In college my alters continued to win academic and leadership awards, enabling their host personality to be named one of twelve outstanding students at a university with an enrollment exceeding 20,000.

They also dated, had many friends, edited magazines professionally, married, had children, and were very active civically—all while the "I," the host personality, was *dead* inside.

The alters carried my entire life capably without anyone noticing anything was amiss—except my husband, who had known me since we were children.

The only area where the alters haven't been completely successful at fooling everyone is in the area of sex and intimacy. That, thus far, is beyond their scope. In fact, that is what contributed to the problems that led me to seek therapy in the first place.

Another disruptive effect attributable to MPD has been forget-fulness.

Although I've always been a forgetful person, I have only "lost time" three times in my life, and that was twenty years ago, due to consuming too much alcohol. I have worked very hard subconsciously to cover up the "forgetfulness" with a highly-organized and compulsive system of list-and-note-making. While this has enabled me to be perceived as a highly-efficient, capable, and organized person, I have lived in fear of losing the lists or notes—for without them, I would remember nothing.

Through therapy I have learned to call on different alters to reveal the information I need, instead of relying solely on the lists.

Now that I'm aware of the existence of alters and how they work, I find that I have to work to monitor who is allowed to speak in times of stress in order to remain appropriate.

On the flip side, the alters, although sometimes demanding and disconcerting, can be called upon at times of stress in the present to help me cope when I am overwhelmed by flashbacks, voices and images from the past. I can ask whomever can handle the situation to step forward, and that alter does so . . . managing the situation quite well with no one realizing it, except, of course, my therapists.

Although multiplicity may be labeled a disorder by the therapeutic community, I consider it a gift from heaven. For without it, I would quite literally be either dead or demented to such a degree as to require permanent institutionalization.

With it, I have been given a set of abilities, potential, and a connection to my Higher Power which I would not otherwise have.

I realize that multiplicity can sometimes be highly difficult for the host personality to live with, but I, for one, would like the therapeutic community to know that I owe my life, my sanity, and the rich quality of my life to my alters.

It seems to me that the general public tends to view people with MPD as being both psychotic and dangerous. TV frequently presents us as axe-murdering, Jekyll and Hyde types. Despite the fact that I have nearly completed my doctorate in psychology, these frightening television images stuck in my mind when I was first diagnosed as having MPD. I was afraid that I might have a murderous monster hidden inside. It was quite a relief to find my "angry monster" was only a little girl who ran away and broke glass when upset.

Currently, I belong to an MPD support group and I am impressed by how ordinary and mundane our members are. We are just hard-working, law-abiding citizens. Many of us are married, have children, attend PTA meetings. We are your neighbors and co-workers. Considering that most of us suffered horrendous abuse in childhood, we are doing rather well at being "normal." I wish there was some way of communicating to the public that MPD is not some esoteric, rare, bizarre condition. It is an all too common survival defense for individuals who, at an early age, had to live through psychologically intolerable conditions. It is defense against insanity. —Deborah S.

One thing that I think is important for everyone to know who deals with a person with MPD—the therapists, friends, family, and self is that there has to be an incredible life force in this person. In the most adverse and diabolical situations, this person was able to create alters within themselves to deal with trauma that others might not survive.

As my story unfolds, I know that I could not have survived what I went through without doing what I did. And those who choose to share in the pain, shame, fear, and suffering of one with MPD, can also share in the rebirth of a human being.

If I were to wish for anything, I would wish for patience for all of those who deal with the disorder; the patient, the therapist, the family, and the friends. Patience in dealing with the kaleidoscope of emotions that they will all be subjected to throughout the recovery process. I also believe that the therapist, family, and friends must have a tremendous amount of energy and resources to help carry the patient along when her strength and resources are depleted, and the trauma becomes too overwhelming. Oftentimes it is only their energy, their resources, and their love that will give the person with MPD a reason to keep fighting one more day. —Jan C.

7

UNIFICATION

A person can be "healthy" without having to integrate all of his or her parts. Integration should be an option, but not the only option, in one's pursuit of mental health and a good life.
—I.R.T.

When I imagine integration, it seems wonderful, painful, thrilling, saddening. I can't tell you what it's like to be whole because I don't remember. I believe it will be wonderful. But you can't explain water to a fish because it knows nothing else. I think it will be like a reweaving of a torn fabric. —Julie W.

I'm Gregory and now I'm almost ten but when my therapist first found us, I was only four and I was afraid all the time that she was going to make me disappear or die.

I wish I'd known right away that I would get better and bigger and she'd teach me lots of things.

Now I even know about integration because I used to be Gregory & George & Jeffrey & George and it wasn't even scary to them to join, it was really nice. And now I'd like to join with some of the others and when they are ready to, maybe we will. So I'm not afraid of having to disappear anymore.

My therapist always told me I could stay, I just didn't really believe her for a long time.

And one of the older ones inside—a *lot* older—doesn't want to write but she says that she wishes a whole lot that she knew when she was diagnosed that it was very *good* that the whole system functioned so well outside that nobody knew she was an MPD. She thought for a long time that it probably meant she wasn't *really* a multiple and it made it hard to believe that bad, bad things happened to us . . . because she never knew and did so well in the outside world.

(See, we kept it *all* a secret from her so nobody would get in trouble with outside grown-ups.)

She was all confused for a long, long time because we didn't act like she thought real multiples acted. Now she's real glad The System is so good in troubled times. —Cindy B.

Only in these last few months of my therapy for MPD did I really understand how the rationing of energy between the personalities affect each of us.

For years, I continued to be frustrated by my inability to sustain activity—it was as if the flow were shut off. Now, I understand that while that energy flow was coming to me, it was at the same time being routed to all the others, thus depleting my energy store much faster than the people around me.

My measurement of the energy available to me did not take into account the fact that others would be drawing on it. My understanding now is that although the other personalities are not "out," it still takes a certain amount of energy for their "maintenance." Not only were my activities curtailed by this, but I spent much time berating myself for being "less than."

If I had had better understanding—perhaps if an analogous situation had been presented to me at an earlier time—what energy I did have available to me would have been more effectively and efficiently spent. —Carol T.

We hate the word integrated. We work as a team and will stay as a team. —R.C.

Integration is something I look forward to, although my parts would take issue with that! But just as the patterns of dissociative behaviors lasted for many, many years, it is understandable to me that it will take a while to unravel the reasons my mind originally "divided."

It will take time to discover the role each of us had to play in our survival. Each part was a victim of traumatic betrayal. As those traumas are given time to heal, I think we will eventually know each other better and finally "come together."—Vickie G.

Uneasy Integration

By Carol T.

I wish a therapist could "know" without having to experience it, the spiralling growth of confusion and disconnection that is a direct result of the discovery and integration of the personalities. Never have I felt so insane as in these last months of my therapy. The disorientation of mind and senses, the inappropriate actions, the hyperactivity leading to utter exhaustion, the inability to focus or concentrate—all let loose by the process of recovery. I understand that these symptoms are side effects of the recovery process, and yet, I must say "the cure is worse than the disease." Only because I believe this is a time-limited condition, and that it will change, can I *force* myself to continue at this point.

And maybe, I not only wish the therapist could "know" the traumatic effect of the ongoing chaos, but I wish the therapist could find a new tool or a new path that would replace at least some portion of this part of the healing. The strength and willingness with which I faced the horror of my past were nothing compared to what I have had to scrape together to survive these side effects of recovery. Yes, the processes of current therapy do provide for functional recovery. But, can we have more?

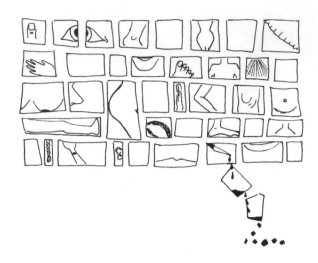

Pieces

Charlene R.

Fragments, scattered like
Broken Glass.
Some edges sharp,
poised
to cut and wound,
to strike out.
Others dull,
no glint,
unpolished
flat
lifeless.

Bouncing and skimming
restless.
This jigsaw
this abstract
this frightened puzzle
is coming together,
the pieces beginning
to fit.

All of Me

By Gregory B.

Said the Caterpillar sternly,
"Explain yourself!"
    "I can't explain myself, I'm afraid sir," said Alice,
"because I'm not myself, you see." (Carroll, Lewis, *Alice in Wonderland*,
NY: Meridian, 1960, p. 67.)

> *I laughed when they told me of MPD.*
> *Or that there is more than one of me. Sybil I think, not me.*
> *That was Friday,*
> *now I am beginning to feel the different parts of me.*
> *Or should I say personas of me.*
> *Or is "states" the better word?*

I find the feeling awkward. Like walking up steps where each stoop
is a different height. Do I step high, or low? Do I bumble along looking
the drunk and dancing man? Do I try to anticipate and fall? At times it is
like waking up in a strange room realizing I'm on a business trip and this
is a hotel. The difference is, in the hotel I remember checking in and
choosing the room. But when meeting myself, I cannot choose the place
or the time. They are stolen moments that sneak up on you like death.

This convergence, this schizoid rendezvous, this grand introduction,
well, it scares me some moments. Once harmless and translucent they
now glow. They run through my house like a screaming woman with a
boiling child. I'm the only one who hears.

They grab me when I open my mouth to sing and hear someone else,
when passing a mirror and I don't recognize who I see or when I quickly
answer the phone and don't understand who said "hello," and what they
mean by it—well, I begin to wonder.

I spend light years wondering.

I am wondering now. Wondering how I am noticing this oddity.
Where did I acquire this skill? Who is it that observes that I am not who
I think I am? Is it me or another part of me. How can I be the observer
and the object observed? Doesn't the self-operating surgeon have to go
under the gas sometime? Who is holding the knife as he sleeps? And as he
dreams, as he chases himself down an alley, around a corner and catches
the running man by the white coat, does he notice it is his own hand on

the back of his collar? Is it just my mind flipping quickly forward and then playing itself back again, back again?

Who am we really and how do I talk about myselves? English has no cupped hands to carry my meaning. Now I must deal with the singular plural. How odd to be something inexpressible in language. To find no tools made to launch my ship. It must be the way Picasso felt, no Van Gogh. To see and not to be able to express. Is that what insanity is? If so, then lucidity is held only in a dictionary and vision only in the sleeping man's mind. But I'm awake as I stand being the reflection of two in the mirror.

Sometimes I get lucky. I catch myselves. Then I am left gawking. When do I catch myselves, if only by the nape of the neck, how do I make myself face each other. I am so different from myself sometimes. Like matter and anti-matter. Am I waiting to bump into the other on some unexpected dark corner? What will be left? Will there be a grand flash of light, pure energy in a moment of space and time, like the forming of some distant sun? Or will I cancel myself out? Will I become a vacuum?

Blank time?

Void?

Darkness?

Can I then only be expressed in the past tense or future tense?

And when one is gone, this Siamese twin I have connected at the mind, will I mourn the loss? Will I visit this man's grave and cry for myself. Or is gone the wrong concept? Is absorption , or metamorphoses better? Is this my time for wrapping up tightly into a cocoon and loosing matter to whirl and fly changing myselves from us to me? Will I find that inside myself I will then be like two taking up the space of only one? Will I be like two billiard balls, a red five and a yellow one laying on the same table in the exact some spot? What a combination that would make, an orange six? What problems that could bring. No wonder billiards are for gambling, all for the color of money!

Color! That's it—color. It must be. Metamorphoses must be like color. The blending. The resolve. A piercing magenta with the frigidity of a cyan, and from the marriage no longer two, but one. The blending of a tangy yellow with a midnight blue bursting forth filling a spring field of tender greens that blow in the wind. One color, one mind—unique on it's own, but the totality of both.

Are these answers? Well it is in the bending that strange patterns whirl. It is in the fusion that unknown hues rage and then die a bit. And in mixing, not even the colors know exactly what they will become.

So as for answers, I will wait and let sparks fly and gases meld. For a creativity is not the arrow meeting the circle. It is the flight. It is in the creating that the magic comes, that the stars cross. It is in the journeying that twists through craggy corridors and mistaken turns that discoveries are made. It is the spilling of yellow in black that olive is made. Creation is like the bringing forth of heavens and oceans. It forces one to dabble a bit, to mix, to blow soft winds upon—to ask what if, and then try.

Yes, allow us to whirl a bit and see where I land.

Affinity

By Kathleen O.

Runaway feelings,
Runaway mind,
Run.
Runaway scared.
Now it's you sitting there,
Being me—
All the time.

Holding pictures,
Holding answers,
Waiting.
Holding time.
Now gently sharing memories,
Embracing me—
Joining fragments in my mind.

Touching,
reaching cautiously
out to each other's
face.

Searching
each one's eyes
looking for hope,
reassurance,
strength
in another's face
to carry us through.

To find
some way
to live in
Peace
Together.

I wish I could find more descriptions of integration. My first layer is integrated and I really don't like it . . . mostly. —Rebecca R.

Who Goes? Who Stays?

By Susan B.

Spouses, friends, and supportive family members must accept the fact that MPD is real. It isn't always like "Sybil." There are varying severities.

I would like them to know how important their understanding, support and patience is. Multiples are not always easy to live with or even to care about, but we are worth it.

MPD is a coping mechanism that usually starts in childhood. Although in adulthood it can become a severe hinderance, we can't just turn it off. We can't just send the others (alters) away. In some cases we love them as good friends. This may be hard to understand, but we have been through a lot together. Alternatively, you may have a favorite that you would love to have "stay" while the others leave. None of us have control of that.

Please understand that we are all part of a whole. We have to come back together to live life as one. No one can tell you or me who that one will be, what she or he will be like. Who he or she will be is there in all the alters, but how the pieces come together is not up to you or me or the therapist.

Please understand that I am as afraid of who she will be as you are. As hard as multiplicity can be to live with, choosing to work toward integration is a painful and frightening process. I would like friends and family members to know that the joining of alters can be like the death of a beloved family member. Although joining is a sign of healing, I still grieve for the loss of a friend who was always there for me.

Time is essential. Integration, fusion, or whatever you choose to call it, must not be rushed. —Lillian F.

Interfering Integrations

By Carole G.

It is a tremendously funny paradox that while most multiples want desperately to be well, they put up a good deal of resistance to getting it done. Integration, although basically an ongoing process, can put a client into a real tailspin, especially if she is not ready.

Early in integration, when the client realizes the alter to be integrated will no longer be accessible, she naturally grieves this loss. Yet as integration progresses, it begins to dawn on the patient that soon all responsibility will fall to *her*.

That is a pretty staggering thought. The integrated personality must now perform all of the tasks previously divided between many personalities.

Integration itself can be experienced in as many ways as there are multiples. For some, aftereffects of a formal integration are limited to headaches, eyeaches, lack of coordination and various other somatic complaints. Integration is so highly individualized that the results can go from those mentioned all the way to near-catatonia.

Consciously, most multiples want to be integrated. But subconsciously, they are terrified.

We Are Family

By Tony B.

For me at least, switching personalities is not like putting on a new suit. Control over who is out at any given time is limited.

Also, I hesitate to call my insiders "personalities," because they are not complete units or mono-persons, capable of a whole range of feelings, experiences, etc.

Instead, I have different "people" to handle all that.

For example, I was not permitted to act like a child, be sad, afraid, etc. That's why one alter is a frightened, sad, six-year-old.

The luxury of being angry, or standing up for myself was denied; now there are two alters that are in charge of those emotions.

On the surface, my alters seem complete. But speak with them for awhile and you realize you are talking to characters in a play. Each alter has his own past, his own narrow band of feelings.

Therapists need to realize that they have been single units (personalities) all their lives. I have been many units all of mine. To blithely speak of merging is frightening. Who will tell me right from wrong? Will I remember how to drive? Play music? What will remain and what do I do to curb the loneliness? Merging is tantamount to saying, "Give up who you know yourself to be. Become empty."

I would like to know more right now about what to expect toward the completion of therapy. After a long, close relationship with therapists, what can I expect to happen to that relationship? What do other therapists and patients feel is appropriate? How good are integrated MPDs at coping after therapy? —Kathy C.

Phases of Integration

By Patsy Q.

I feel therapists should know that all of "us" are unique and not necessarily something evil to be disposed of. In working with me, my therapists were considerate of each one's feelings and treated us all with compassion.

In my case, integration became a life/death situation; therefore, I had a long hard battle for over a period of six years to integrate.

Therapists and clients should know that even after a "successful" integration, there is *no* guarantee that dissociation will not recur. It has for me. Now I have accepted the fact, that like an addict, *once a multiple— always one.*

Also, I think therapists should know that a multiple needs to feel worthwhile at some stage in life. Often I feel totally useless or feel I am handicapped and can never lead a "normal" life.

Being different doesn't always make you feel "special." A lot of times you long to be the *same.*

Commit?

By Margaret O.

The more "sane" I get, the crazier I feel.
    Because I feel!
The walls I had built before kept the crush
    of reality away.
Now it closes in and closes in.
    and closes in.

I watch it filtering through my body
    Ripping, tearing, soiling
       . . . and cleansing?

I watch it get closer
    I know I am vulnerable.
I do not feel panic.
    It seems so inevitable.

So I stand stripped
    . . . naked . . .
      to the elements of life.
There is no rapture.
There is no bitterness.
No great expectations.
No seething fury.
Just me . . . standing before fate.

But always with a choice
    for myself
by myself
    of myself.

I do not wish to commit death
But, oh how hard it is to commit life!

FRIENDS AND
FAMILIES

*I wish that my friends and family could under-
stand the nature of being multiple. It is just as
frustrating to switch as to watch (actually more
so). Switching is not done to avoid things, but
rather in response to fear. It is not a deliberate
act meant to offend. People get upset. I wish they
would understand this is my coping mechanism.
I am trying to change it. I didn't pick it for the
hell of it. I chose it in order to survive.*
—*Kitty R.*

Questions for significant others:

—What makes you frightened of a dissociative state? Is it a feeling of powerlessness or fear?

—When someone you love is acting differently (being a teenager or a child), how do you feel? Are you able to still see the person?

—What would help you to feel more at ease?

—Are you willing to read about MPD to understand how the person continues to survive?

—Lastly, will you share gentle compassion? We do need and will heal with this gift. The cost is heartrending. —Grace R.

For those involved with MPD patients, there are two things that they must understand to be of help. First, that MPD does exist and produces a great deal of confusion for the patient. Second, MPD is an extension of a normal device used by everyone to some degree at some time. Defense mechanisms are normal and protective. The individual with MPD has simply employed the most extreme mechanism, dissociation, to survive a life threatening experience. We are not "crazy" and can become healthy with time and help. —Lillian F.

181

Families should not ask for *facts*. There are no facts or proof. Emotion and fear should be facts enough. Support and love *whomever* is out. They need love even if you don't know them very well. —R.C.

Family members should know that we're learning whole new ranges of emotions, and because they're new, they may be overdone. I am learning to express anger but it is so hard that at times I'm overemphatic. The same with sadness, etc. Hopefully, practice will make perfect. —Anne M.

I would like the people in my life to respect my journey into wholeness. Although they don't need to know the specific details of the events in my childhood, they should know that the events went far beyond their wildest nightmares.

In many ways, I lived a concentration camp existence . . . but my perpetrators were not unknown guards. My perpetrators were trusted, beloved family members. What they did to me was not random torture. I was singled out for worse.

I want people in my life to know I survived a hell almost beyond imagination. I want them to know that I am angry beyond measure and that when *anyone* denies the pain inflicted daily on children, I want to tear down walls and scream! I am not an isolated case. There are many, many of us "out there."

I want people in my life to respect me. I feel as if my endurance alone commands respect. I want praise for my efforts; I want cheerleaders in my life. I want gentle people to *be* with me and the children who live inside me. And I want to re-learn what love and care are really about.

I have a sneaking suspicion that what I was taught was wrong.

Lastly, I do not want to journey alone. My friends and family may sometimes feel inadequate to help me. I feel inadequate, too. But to have a friend along on the journey is the sweetest gift possible.

I ask my friends and family to not shut me out. Although my reality is different from yours, we have much to learn from each other.
—Grace R.

I wish my friends and family to know that this is not an amusing game of guessing who's "out" on a particular occasion, or wondering which alter did what. When I shyly say that I've got to go do something childish for the Kids, I'm not joking. I *do* have to tend to their needs. —Suzanne D.

I think family members need to work on co-dependence. My husband has greatly improved in this and this has really helped me to be able to integrate my adult self(s) and be more assertive.

I think if they know why things seem to "always" go wrong at certain times or in certain experiences, they can let up on themselves and their expectations.

It helps when my husband is patient, rolls with the punches, lets go of my reactions.

It helps me when he and other significant others ask me who I am, point out when I'm different so we can discuss it. I'm becoming more aware. My husband is saying, "I don't feel comfortable with this person," or "You're not hearing things the way I mean them."

Or he takes me in his arms and says, "I know it's hard. Just relax and maybe you can get into a better place." —Dorothy R.

At Least We're Not Boring

By Susan C.

Spouses need to be very patient with MPDs just as MPDs need to be very patient with spouses.

Spouses need to know that they are loved, but maybe not in the same way by all parts. I do believe it is as confusing to the spouse as the spouse is to the multiple. Couples should be in therapy together.

The spouse, friends, family, and therapist need to be aware that even in silence there may be some very intense activity or talking going on internally. It is all right to ask about what is going on inside.

Friends should be picked carefully. The host personality should listen carefully to internal opinions as to who your friends should be. (The host need not agree.)

I do not think all of my friends could tolerate seeing parts of me. I have lost friends just over the news that I am a multiple. So, the few who do get to see parts of me are picked very carefully and are very supportive.

Others should talk to alters just as they would anyone else. Remember multiples have access to a lot of information. Treat them with respect yet be mindful of their age.

Persons with MPD are very intuitive and can usually pick up on insincerity. Be consistent with them. We like to be able to trust people enough to feel safe when asking questions.

Being a multiple is painful and complicated at best . . . though it does have its humorous moments, too. Please be mindful that this is not an overnight healing process. Just like growing up, it takes time.

Caring Information

By Grace Rose

I do believe that spouses, close friends, (and maybe some family members) need to know our diagnosis . . . but not everything. I feel it is safe to share it all in therapy and to check out with our doctor what is appropriate to tell others. But I do feel people need practical information about MPD and the dissociative states one might be in at times (little child, teenager, artist, etc.) They should know not to overwhelm the person if terrified alters come out.

I usually need rest and space . . . not people hovering over me.

I also feel that the people we live with need to know this information so that they feel safe and understand. It goes two ways; survivors and pro-survivors feeling safe.

My spouse and friends should know they do not have to (and probably shouldn't) relate to, support, and get to know all of my alters. I want them to relate to *me* . . . an adult "all-one-people." They don't need the burden, and I don't want to be seen as fragmented more than necessary. *Accept* my alters, but be *my* friend or spouse. —Kim B.

Understanding

By Caitlin M.

I have discovered that for people with integrated personalities, it is very difficult for them to make sense of the way MPD works.

First, I wish they could understand that although they are talking to "me," many alters are watching them all the time and may have thoughts and opinions much different than mine. If they knew this, perhaps they would not be so surprised.

Also, MPD takes a lot of emotional plasticity for supportive friends and spouses, because alters vary in what they need. I wish others understood that such patience, willingness to be surprised, and understanding, are most helpful for those of us with MPD.

They should know I am very timid of intimacy, having been so dreadfully betrayed in my childhood. Many alters get frightened, act rude, run away, manipulate, vanish, act coy, lie, etc., at the first glimpse of intimacy.

I hope my supportive fold understands that this is not personally related to them but comes from my own internal terror. Each alter is behaving in ways that she has learned were appropriate in the past. This might reduce personal frictions.

I wish supportive friends could know I want the intimacy but am terrified, and I frequently re-enact the strong need to hide.

It helps me a lot when my friends understand that "I" am never completely in control of my life, that I constantly have flashbacks, or am triggered by something ordinary into a memory of some childhood hell.

Sometimes friends feel guilty when this happens. I wish they understood it was not their fault; the trauma reaction may be triggered by the present "reminder," but the source of pain is from long ago.

Sometimes friends think I am "weird" because I suddenly start acting differently, or become unable to wear certain clothes or do some things.

An especially difficult problem for me is that the thoughts or feelings I express on the surface are only a small part of the whole. I was well-programmed by the cult I grew up in to look and act "normal" while in fact responding to all their obedience training. So when I look the most "together" and "functional" is often when I am the most desperate.

I want to feel more directly; I want to express how I really feel, but I can't.

I wish friends did not take some of my "moods" at face value, for my complete feelings cannot all be there.

It is also really important to me that friends be consistent, supportive, and honest. Because of MPD, I'm never sure if I've done a thing well, or offended somebody. The more friends understand my vast insecurity and confusion about ordinary life matters which they can take for granted, the better off we'll be.

185

Many alters just can't understand or do sophisticated things. They make mistakes. If my friend understands that it comes from confusion or a young alter, or perhaps an angry, left-out one, then the mistake makes sense.

And although child alters might like it, I wish friends could know that it is not a good idea to treat those alters as babies or to "mother" me, although they may speak and participate in a relationship. The latter is fine; the former breeds dependency.

I appreciate friends who are able and willing to talk with alters who want to participate; friends who are not frightened.

More than anything, I wish supportive friends to know that I am reaching to them in the ways I can, at the pace I can. I am not weird because of MPD, nor am I to be pitied for it.

I am struggling with many realities at once and trying to live in a world that I don't always feel is mine. I've been terribly betrayed and have trouble expressing my love; often I'm in too much pain to participate with others.

But I'm still here, as best as I can be.

I still don't know if I can ever fully trust enough to have a loving relationship with a man. —Anne M.

Who Am I?

By Sarah F.

A friend asks, "How do I know which one you are? Is this you?"

Who am I?

Does it matter so much? Am I a combination of what you see, what I feel, my past as well as my present?

I am a multiple. I am not like any other multiple nor any other person. We all share common ground, but I am me, just as you are you. I am more than some would contend. I am unique. I am a human being, and human beings are unique.

Each personality helps me to be me, just who I am, unhealed, integrated, or fused. I am the sum of all my parts.

I need outside nourishing. Certainly, no one taught me to nourish myself. When I am sad, lonely, overwhelmed, or hopeless, I turn to you, often, with few boundaries. You are my therapist, my father, my confessor. I am your client, your child, your sister, yet we are never friends.

No one has discovered so much of me nor helped in my self-discovery with such dimension. I trust you like few others, still I am consistently testing. My past demands it.

I am child, I am adult and all that lies between. I bear the burdens,

187

the pain and the secrets of past generations. My suffering continues, yet diminishes, as I give up their burdens to the outside world.

My personalities are the blessings of my past. They helped me to survive, to live, to be. What each secretly carried grew harder and harder to hold and needed to be put down.

Today, my personalities are the miracles of my present—each holding on to some talent, some memory, some something that will help make me whole. As I have learned to love my "people," I am learning to love, to value, myself.

Often I am confused, hurt, happy or angry, and with what seems like emotion beyond comprehension, beyond what pens can write or spoken words express; so strong that no measurement is large enough.

Each day I labor to give birth to myself. I am beginning to feel my feelings. It is important that you (my family, my friends, my therapist) care, try, are there when it is possible and are consistent.

It is important that I try, that I work, and that I accept all that I am, all that I have been, and all that I can be. To walk this path alone seems impossible.

For all the people who have ever said I have switched to have companions inside—I wish they could feel the devastating loneliness that I live.
—Anne M.

"T" and Me

By Patsy Q.

I am lucky. I have some special people in my life who have stood by me— one being my "spouse." T has given me love and support . . . and often had every reason to leave.

Others should know that life with a multiple is extremely difficult, but patience goes a long way. At times we can't explain certain things, so maybe if they would learn more about multiple personality and not hide it as if it were a disease, then they could learn to live with us instead of living in fear of us.

My immediate family kept me a secret until they had no control anymore and I think that hurt worst of all. I had a father who called me "crazy" and a mother who, out of fear, pampered me to the point that I became an emotional cripple as well.

I think if they had known and understood more about my problem, things in my life would have been different and I wouldn't be incarcerated today.

They should also know that we are all looking for the same things they are: love, peace, happiness, and a place in society. There should be more T's in the world.

We want to say to loved ones that we're sorry. We never realized until recently how much frustration, anger and pain the diagnosis causes others.

My nineteen year-old son has lived with me being in and out of hospitals since he was eight—even though this diagnosis was just recently made. It's just been in the last year that I've learned how strongly this affected him. None of us can change that.

This is as painful, if not more so, than any other part of the diagnosis. —Virginia C.

Spouses really need a support group. They should be able to be a part of therapy, when appropriate, and not shunned.

I think it is important, that they know what to do when something triggers us. My husband (now ex-husband) was good in that area. He knew how to talk with whomever was present. It made him feel like a part of the healing. He appreciated it.

But, his ability to talk to alters was also a hindrance. He used it against me when we were separating.

As for family, friends and relatives, I would *never* in a lifetime tell them. I hear their opinions about mental health and MPD. They feel MPD is demon possession and "they would *never* go near anyone that had it!" So, I keep my mouth shut.

It is sad that I can't share with them. It has put an end to seeing them. I'm so afraid of a part coming out and being rejected.

And yet, it is hard being lonely too. —Diana R.

Those with supportive friends and family are fortunate. Supportive people are great and should be given a pat on the back. I'd just encourage them to be patient and never ridicule or laugh at parts that may come out.

It's very important to be treated as an adult, allowing you to be a part of them. It hurts to be treated differently, or excluded, or to feel that friends are wary of alters. It's best to act naturally.

I know that I am really sensitive and want to be treated with dignity and respect. I would also tell supportive friends and relatives, that the diagnosis of MPD should stay among themselves. Gossiping may cause damage or keep a person with MPD from a job, a family, etc . . . . because many people don't understand it. —Myra H.

If You Walked in Our Shoes . . .

By Julie for twenty-three others

I wish people knew how difficult it is to live this way. Sometimes things get really confusing. Especially when you get calls and letters from people you don't even know, or find yourself in a place that you don't know.

It's hard to put anything down on paper because nine times out of ten you don't finish. You get a thought in your mind and it doesn't make any sense because it isn't yours to begin with. You find clothes in your house that aren't yours.

The worst distraction is that you constantly hear the alters in your head. They may not be talking to you but you can still hear them.

People should not be scared of our alters. If they do get to know them, they will be learning more about the person they love. Do not be afraid or ashamed of us. What we have is not catching. Accept us as people, because that is what we are. Learn as much as you can about MPD. It will make you feel a lot better.

Finally, remember: if you are scared of a person who has MPD, imagine how that person feels. It's scary for us, too!

I need my friends to know:

—I am not crazy or weird, but sufficiently strong and creative to split off from the abuse, allowing a stronger child inside of me to handle the trauma at that time.

—Although the abuse occurred in the past, I relive every experience as if it were now. The trauma, terror, and pain must be experienced now to overcome the power of the past.

—I can make it! But, I need love, support, and patience. I know you don't want me to hurt any more or experience anymore pain or memories from the past. You want this to be over and done with, but my only hope of future happiness and fulfillment lies in facing and overcoming the pain of my past. —Julie W.

Please, friends and family, don't tease us! We really are sensitive.

Please do not desert us.

Make sure things are written on the calendar so we can remember all of our extra responsibilities.

It is not a fun game to be called out just to be used!

We are *not* moody.

When you accuse us of having said or done something, our denials are serious. We do not remember everything. —Barbara G.

Those close to us should know that treatment may extend for a prolonged period of time. This doesn't mean the patient isn't working hard enough. The journey involves phases of growth as well as (seemingly) total remission.

Be patient with us, and don't ask, "How much longer is this going to take?" or "When are you going to let go of the past?"

Most of us have lived with this pain since early childhood. We may not even have discovered that abuse took place until mid-adulthood. We are growing from infancy in many ways. Please be patient. —Carol T.

I want my family members and friends to know:

—That alters are not there to hurt them but to protect me from harm.

—My alters would hurt me before hurting others (via self-abuse, etc.).

—That I am not *crazy* but functional.

—How to respond to alters. —Nancy G.

I think friends should know the importance of loyalty. They need to know you are not just one, but have other personalities who need to feel safe also. Keeping your word is important in establishing trust. —Marsha C.

What I wish my spouse had known:

> How time consuming MPD treatment is.
>
> That people don't make up MPD.
>
> That the prognosis is excellent.
>
> That having opposite sex alters is the norm.
>
> That each alter really thinks he/she is an independent being.
>
> That many new abilities will be discovered.
>
> That my experience would enrich her own life. —Charlie Anderson

The only thing I can say to spouses, friends, and supportive family members, is to stick by your multiple.

So much pain and fear is involved that the multiple may act weird, or even irrational, at times.

Being a multiple isn't easy. There is no way to explain the time lapses, the "forgotten" conversations, the misplaced things, the "disappearing" when you had no idea where we were.

There is no way to ever make up to you the bad times we've had. Please, remember the good times and hopefully they will outweigh the others.

Be patient with the multiple person in your life. Love us for who we are. —Terry J.

I hope my loved ones know:

> —It's ok for us to play, especially when the little ones are around: to go into toy stores, own a teddy bear, or doll, or any toy.
>
> —We get incredibly frustrated.
>
> —It's not safe for us to tell you about the others and our past and our world. We have to be a fake.
>
> —U.F.O. (that's me—Unbelievably Freaky Opportunity).

—MaryLou P.

What should others know about MPD?

> All that they want to know.

Give a person what can be handled and digestion goes smoothly. Force feed significant others and they'll vomit all over the carpet for sure. —Wendy W.

I am a multiple with a family. It has been a very difficult road for me and for them. I feared telling and worried that if I did, I wouldn't be loved.

In the beginning, when I would not tell my husband anything, he was confused and angry with me and my doctors. After he knew, he still loved me and became actively involved in my treatment. So many things made sense to him that he no longer felt shut out.

Sharing the diagnosis was hard because I felt I would lose the love I had. Keep advising MPDs to share with mates. It improves the quality of therapy, of life, and builds the support system. His help with young alters helps keep transference for them at a more manageable level. —Kathy C.

Others should know, first, that we who have MPD are not crazy—but we are scared that we are.

Second, we may be the best, most exciting friend they ever had. Because we have to explore our souls, we are thinking, feeling people as well as triggered, dissociated people. Our friendship will never be shallow.

For support family members, if you don't share the memories, recognize that distance is necessary for both of you so you neither deny the recovering person, nor force your own process. Spouses—get into a CODA (Co-Dependents Anonymous) group. —Rebecca R.

I'd like people to know I am still one person. I am sensitive, but also aware of the need to instill some humor to the situation. I hope they would feel free to know they could approach me with questions, and perhaps tell me which of my alters they have talked with. —Martha H.

I prefer friends and family do not keep secrets from me. If I do something that isn't like me, let me know. Don't cover up or overlook things. People with MPD need to know precisely how they relate to others (more than how they "think" they relate). Friends and family must not take any *abusive* behavior from MPDs.

Try taking life one day at a time, but broken into smaller minutes. That's how I get through the day. —Amie R.

Spouses, friends, and others should realize that we are just trying to survive the best way we can. We have to learn new ways to cope, other than MPD. —Will R.

People who care need to know that MPD *is* curable. There *is* hope. But it takes time.

It took my husband a *long* time to stop putting pressure on me to finish therapy. We were struggling financially and therapy put the final crunch on our budget. This made it very difficult to just relax and work on things as they came up in therapy.

For weeks I felt I *had* to make a major stride every time I set foot in my therapist's office. It was very hard to learn that healing comes in its own time—with its own natural pace. Trying hard and commitment *are* important . . . but rushing through the integration process is simply not possible. —Lori B.

Do not give your all, for people with MPD will take it.

Being a good role model will teach a multiple to parent his or her own system. This is a priceless gift.

If anyone feels a need to give a multiple anything, give it from the heart. For the one you give it to might not be the one who you want to have it.

More so, do not expect gratification from the one who is receiving. Take inventory of what you have to offer and don't give more than you can afford.

Be patient. It is hard work and we're worth it. —Sharon A.

I wish people understood that switching is not always intentional or avoidable, especially in the beginning of treatment. —Julie W.

Information, Please

By MEs

—Family members should be informed of the severity of abuse required to cause MPD. I would have educational information sessions for family members where MPD clients could attend if they wanted to.

—Family members should be knowledgeable of the symptoms of this disorder and of the high recovery rate.

—Family members ought to learn what kind of questions are safe to ask. Safe questions include: "How did you find out about having MPD?" "How do you feel about having MPD?" "What do you want me to know?" "Is there some way I can help you?" These are very helpful and supportive. An unsafe question is, "How many personalities are there?"

—It would be helpful for family members to learn about the effect of abuse on families (and not just on individuals with MPD). MPD, in and of itself, has its own effect on families.

—The people close to me should know that I am not a weak person or a coward and that I do not want pity. Some of the basic personality characteristics of people like me are: intelligence, creativity, strong survival instinct, and a very strong character. We are feeling people, we are courageous, and we have an inner drive that is inextinguishable.

—I wish that literature was available for clients and family members about MPD. It would be less threatening to me to know what exposure those close to me have had about my disorder. I might learn from reading literature written for families, too.

To all of you who care about us, thank you for your support. You have taught us that not all of the world is violent and cruel—an invaluable lesson.

We would like you to know that:

1) MPD is not contagious. You cannot catch it, and spending time with a multiple will not make you crazy.

Spending time with a multiple may push you to examine your own life, your views, and your perception of people. However, self-reflection is very different from being crazy.

2) My people are here to help me . . . not to hurt you. Don't be afraid of us. We are just people. Some of the things we say or do may appear to be very confusing and coming from out of nowhere. The truth is that everything we do or say has a reason. Be patient and together we will discover those reasons.

3) If there are a hundred people in a room, you are not going to like everybody. The same applies to us. You are not going to like all of us. We know that. All we ask is that you accept all of us. If you can't, please be honest and say so.

4) There are benefits to knowing a multiple. It gives you a good excuse to play. We love to ride carousels, fly kites, etc. So please, join us. It is a special part of our healing that we love to share with others.

—Annette K.

Family Consequences

By Kathy A.

Our family members include a husband . . . which no one at this point remembers getting. (He is very supportive but we are as strangers.) Three children live with us. (We have lost three others to adoption, foster care, and a residential long term treatment center.)

The children who live here have been told of the diagnosis. For one child it all made sense. Another child wanted to run away from us.

For the youngest child, our resident author wrote a beautiful story about a little boy and . . . I think he understood. Since then he seems very relaxed and comfortable around most of us.

It helped them to know we aren't a stranger that hatched overnight but people they had known all along and had generally been comfortable with.

They needed to be told the diagnosis, for it explained so much for them: the inconsistencies they had felt over their lifetimes, the many questions that before had gone unanswered. Their lives became understandable. They knew they weren't crazy for being so confused all the time.

Above all, it helps the whole family to be able to be light about MPD and to laugh at it sometimes. (Like the time ten of us got into the zoo for the price of one.) It makes it not quite so scary and overwhelming for all of us when we laugh.

Dealing With Difficulties

By Louise H.

Living with MPD is very difficult for everyone involved. Extreme mood swings and behavior changes make life very difficult. If those who are supportive and close to the person are aware of potential problems, and know how to deal with them, life will be easier for all. Suggestions towards this goal include:

a) MPD patients are not always aware of their behavior and what they are saying. For instance, they may think that they are sad, but are really acting angry and disruptive.

b) Many personalities may surface, and each one acts differently.

c) MPDs do not adjust to change easily.

d) MPDs are frightened by many common things and often they do not know why.

e) MPDs may seek out situations that are comfortable but harmful.

f) They can have extreme anxiety attacks when situations represent or remind them of a past abuse.

g) They need to be taught trust, and the therapist is the main teacher.

h) They must never be lied to or have the truth hidden. Even if the truth hurts, everyone must be honest with them.

i) If you're going to be supportive, invest reasonable amounts of consistent time in doing so. But do not promise more than you can deliver. When a supportive person withdraws, it is extremely painful to the patient.

k) People with MPD are very insecure.

l) A person with MPD may be highly functional in one area, but this is not necessarily true for all areas of their lives.

People who know someone with MPD should feel free to talk about it, or ask questions, and be interested. The worst things are being afraid to mention it and pretending it doesn't exist. —Cindy B.

Don't mock the personalities because that pushes them back into hiding, and the healing process will take longer. It is like being abused again. And don't call them crazy, even in jest. —Jo Anne M.

Twelve-Step Programs have been helpful to my family, to help us all know the rules about feelings, etc. My husband comes into my therapy sessions once in a while when he needs understanding or better cooperation from my parts. My therapist was able to facilitate this. My friends who know my diagnosis are very supportive. They call my attention to talk shows, clip articles, and ask questions. —Marcia L.

I would like friends and family to know that during therapy, we are vulnerable. We need time, understanding, and space. —Tony B.

We Want You to Care

By Linda B. (& Friends)

I wish my family would ask more questions about the diagnosis. Most family members are afraid and won't talk about it. They should set up appointments with the therapist to express some of their fears, so that they can be supportive to the afflicted family member or friend.

When I am with my family and am aware that a change is taking place, I leave, because they will not know what to do. I feel isolated and afraid. I neither want to embarrass them nor do I want them to be afraid of me.

I would like to tell my friends and family that I have been here a long time. I have talked with them before. Now they don't want to talk to me. (Heather)

I want to tell them to love Linda and get to know all of us—we are her, we just are different parts. She is still the same person. She wants to die because you do not understand her. Thank God she has her therapist to talk to. We all know her therapist will help us to help her to like herself, and want to live. (Smitty)

I want to show them my drawings. (Annie)

I want to tell them to stay out of her life and leave us alone. There is too much pain because of them. (Shannon)

For friends and family members: Don't feel bad that you didn't figure out I had MPD earlier. I'm still the same person who has been keeping you off balance for years. And as I grow more coherent within myselves, I won't really change, but I might be easier to understand.

I will still love you and need you.

From you I need someone I can trust, so I can learn to trust. I need gentleness, so that my hurts will heal. I need your rage at the injustice of child abuse, so that I can believe my own rage. I need you to be yourself, so I can learn to be myselves. —Cynthia S.

I think family, spouses, and supportive friends should know that remembering is hard to do. Often there will be pain, fear, anger, and lots of confusion. We need their patience, support, love, understanding, and time. Mostly . . . we need time. —Kathy O.

I would like friends to know that they really can't understand MPD. When I need someone to talk to, I like them to listen. That's all. Attempting to explain what it's like to be is just that, an attempt. Two reasons why: they've never been an MPD and I've never *not* been an MPD. —Nathan

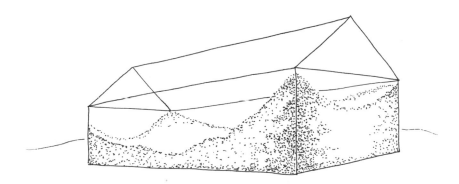

My home was the Sahara,
Dead sand shifting so rapidly
Not even a cactus could grow.
—Ann H.

Guidelines for Friends

By J. Robert

In most respects, We are the only family our host truly possesses. However, I can address those who have formed or may attempt to form friendships with a multiple. A number of guidelines are:

a) If you are not a multiple, do not feign to be one. Merely reading accounts of MPD is not sufficient with regards to understanding what a multiple endures. To believe that one can understand or imitate the realm of multiplicity via such written passages is similar to one believing her/himself cognizant of the complexities of a fission reactor simply by virtue of comprehending a high school physics text.

b) If you are unfortunate enough to witness the ill-conceived actions of an alternate, do not confront the host as if it were her/his sole fault that the alternate in question exercised poor judgment. If the host could control her/his alternates, she/he most certainly would. It is far more advisable to confront the offending alternate and address her/his behavior while said alternate is still present.

The more a host is personally blamed for the shameful acts of an alternate, the less likely it is a host will seek to contact or merge with that alternate. The host may even develop an attitude of hatred towards an alternate whose only offense is an incapacity to properly address either terror or blind rage born out of past trauma.

c) Many have wrongly assumed that if a malevolent alternate exists that the host (or even the entirety of the individual) should be regarded as dangerous. This is an example of black/white thinking. Would it not be erroneous to assume the host to be as benign as her/his most delightful alternate? With that in mind, one might clearly see how equally erroneous it would be to label the host as presently possessing the worst qualities of her/his more unsavory alternates.

In closing, We encourage all who befriend a multiple to consider the task seriously. When one befriends a multiple, one is not merely extending kindness to an individual; one is truly opening arms to an entire family.

I wish my family, as well as the general public, accepted the fact that this disorder exists. People need to be aware of MPD just as they have become aware of Schizophrenia, Manic Depressive Illness, Obsessive-Compulsive Disorder and the other "understandable" mental health disorders.

People need to understand there is nothing exciting or glamorous about MPD. —Patricia R.

My spouse, friends, and family need to earn my trust and respect my disclosures. The process is most devastating as well as draining to all people involved with MPD. It is analyzed and glorified in many books but no one tells these people how to *live* daily with a multiple. There are no directions about what to do with issues of trust, suicide, sex, communication.

The folks who know and have known me feel my boundaries and sense my awesome pain. They realize that they are outside of my experience and can only hope to witness some aspects of my reality.

Family members need to be careful about being attached to certain personalities. Mistrust, vulnerability, disclosure, and *over*exposure of each person involved in the process must be respected at all costs.

The "whole" people around the multiple need to often display and disclose their reality to encourage the multiple to seek collaboration. —Serena

If you care about a person who has MPD, be as honest as you can in the relationship, especially about feelings. We can feel when something is up, but when that awareness is denied it makes us feel more crazy. Realize too that a person with MPD doesn't have all of the answers about this problem. It's going to be a long, hard road. —Diana D.

As for friends, I do not have many. I have only a few (three?) close friends with whom I am comfortably able to share all that goes with this diagnosis.

I wish more of my friends could accept what has happened to me (or simply that *something* terrible has happened to me). I wish they were kind and understanding. I wish they would get to know my alters and not be afraid.

My alters are afraid of outsiders, which is understandable, but if made to feel wanted, they might allow themselves to be known. Then there would be less secrecy and I would be less worried about people finding out. —Celeste P.

A Whole Truth

By Cathy F.

MPD is a method of survival. We who are multiple have learned to adapt to almost any situation. It's the nature of our condition. Naming the condition does not negate its effectiveness, even if the naming comes as a shock to the person being diagnosed. We'll adapt to that information. We'll roll it around, collectively, until we understand what it means for us.

Our experience has been that spouse, friend, and supportive family members, when they have been informed of the diagnosis, seem to watch us carefully and listen carefully as though waiting for us to explode into tiny pieces.

They seem to expect that somehow we are going to change in some significant way and they won't recognize us any more. Or they think we will "go crazy" after finding out and switch from alter to alter until we're exhausted.

In short, they wait anxiously for profound and debilitating changes.

But that has already happened. Our condition allowed us to adapt to the most painful of lives; we have already "gone crazy"; we have already exploded into tiny pieces; we've been switching from alter to alter for years.

There will be no dramatic external change. However, there will be internal turmoil. The truth has been told; now we know, the therapist knows, and any of the above-mentioned close ones know. We've never heard the truth before . . . not the whole truth.

MPD is a whole truth.

As we get our chance, the alters will, one at a time, tell *why* MPD. And as that begins to happen, there will be some very unsettling times as we begin to have co-consciousness about the secrets too horrible to remember in one piece.

We will need quiet time, without being stared at, to focus inward into the cacophony of voices all clamoring to tell, blame, argue, deny, comfort, reject, agonize, and justify what we each have to tell.

But we won't break. Don't keep looking at us as if we can't take care of ourselves, or like we're going to turn into a werewolf or something. All that has already happened. Our task now is to put Humpty Dumpty back together again.

We need support, not smothering attention. We need peace not solicitousness. We need to see your tears and sadness, but we may not be able to, or want to, react to them. Sometimes we will be happy (as though nothing has happened). We'll need space to be happy, too. Sometimes we will be one giant (or infinitesimal) ball of sorrow and heartrending grief. We need those times, too.

Asking questions is fine. Sometimes the answer will be hostile or angry, or sad, or spiteful, or despairing. Those feelings may appear directed at you: but you are only a clear, present, and proximate target. Even if you abused us also, most of the hostility stems from the past. Your abuse was a by-product of the past.

Your kindness is the most healing activity you can engage in. We may not recognize it. We may appear to reject it. We may seem to ignore it. But reform takes a long time inside. Someone(s) is hearing, seeing, feeling the kindness, and eventually you will see, hear, feel in return that we acknowledge that kindness.

Gradually, as we begin to trust your support and kindness, our interaction with you will meld with the healing process. We will learn kindness, caring, and love from you and we will begin to return them.

9

OTHERS' VOICES

Children of the Morning

Will anybody ever see the shame?
And will the siblings ever look back?
Under the shadows of barkless trees
With red, red shards of memory.

Nightmares of beatings past
And hydro wire frayed with use.
A frenzied bestial religion
Whose name is Authority and Mother.

Children of the morning—you are divided.
You're hateful of yourself and all victims.
Yet the scars and scabs still exist
And cannot be swept under the river.

For the current is relentless
Under your pillow—over the night.
In the mirror you come to the only evidence;
The only proof that you are still alive.

Written by A.M.F.
Son of an MPD Patient

Growing With a Partner Who Has MPD

By Elizabeth M.

Living with someone who experiences MPD has changed, enriched, and deepened my life. She is wonderful in many ways. She is one of the most creative people I've ever met.

Living with a person with MPD demands integrity on the part of the significant other. A person with MPD will mirror those parts of yourself that need work. If you accept the challenge to change, they will accept nothing short of your best effort.

My significant other has had an inspiring effect on my personal growth. It is impressive to observe her struggle with values clarification, and to watch as she strengthens herself in the areas of love versus hate, consistency versus being scattered, trust versus fear, and hope versus hopelessness—to name just a few.

I do not see my partner's experience as a lot different from my own, but sometimes I can see it clearer. It helps me understand my own experience.

Understanding multiplicity has also taught me lessons about the universe as a whole. The community within the mind of the multiple reflects the community-at-large in many ways.

We co-parent a child. Seeing my partner struggle to "stop the abusive pattern" demands respect and admiration. She works daily to change thought patterns, beliefs, and responses to the child on the outside, even as those are being changed within.

This choice of a partner has been the right choice for me; your situation may be different.

I suggest that significant others look within themselves for answers when problems arise in "the relationship." MPD may not always be the reason for the relationship dilemma. In fact, MPD may become the scapegoat for areas of personal weakness and immaturity in the "normal" partner. Issues such as sexual identity, trust, boundaries, balance of power within a relationship, and mutual respect for one another require growth in all relationships. Dependency and parental issues are other common trouble-spots. These are key areas of concern and conflict for someone who enters a relationship to be "taken care of"—particularly if the person happens to have MPD.

I would encourage persons with MPD to engage only in relationships that are healthy and loving. I would also encourage significant others to look past behavior to intent, and past fear to strength and wisdom.

Persons with MPD are survivors of the greatest degree. As a society, we have a great deal to learn from them. It has been said that relationships "sand us down to the core of our divinity," and I believe it! Reaching that core is a personal goal of mine for this lifetime. My partner is helping me achieve it.

I would suggest that significant others get a good therapist who will consider the *strengths* of the relationship, rather than questioning the relationship in a knee-jerk fashion.

If there is quality in your relationship, build on it. If it reproduces abuse, change it, or get out of it immediately. Much prayer, work, and sweat go into our relationship. I wouldn't have it any other way.

I would like to share with friends and family members of individuals with MPD that there's not much that you can do to help that person change. However, you can be there for them.

Living with an individual who has MPD is always interesting. It may seem that you just can't take anymore, but do not give up. Do whatever you can to help and support them. I've found several things helpful.

First, the significant other should find some type of support group for him or herself.

Next, it helps to understand that your friend or partner is "departmentalized." The sum of the alter personalities really make up that person. Even with this understanding, it is most helpful to learn how to tell the alters apart, and to deal with each one as an individual.

Finally, you must take every opportunity to help dispel the myths, and try to educate yourself and the general public about MPD.

I would like to see therapists and doctors make more of an attempt to keep "significant others" informed of the progression/regression of their friend or partner. We usually have no idea of what is really going on in therapy, and even the patient may not know what his/her therapy status is. If the patient suffered from some other type of illness (such as cancer), medical professionals would make sure that we were kept fully abreast of the condition.

In this situation, therapists often deny spouses access to information based on the "Doctor/Patient" confidentiality clause. In my experience, the therapist will only involve a partner if his/her life (or someone else's) is in danger. This seems too limited to me. I realize that confidentiality is important, however, we who are close to the patient may be able to offer some helpful insight.

From my side, I have always left the communications option open between my partner's therapist and myself. I know if there was some communication between us, we could probably help each other. —Steven P.

My Wife Has Multiple Personality Disorder

By David M.

More and more is being written about Multiple Personality Disorder (MPD) from the standpoint of the therapist, psychiatrist, or the patient herself. But, as the husband of a bright young woman who has just recently been diagnosed with MPD, I have found very little literature telling me what I am going to experience during the process of my wife's recovery. There are presently only a handful of treatment units nationwide, and practically no support groups for spouses.

I thought it appropriate, therefore, to discuss some of the issues which I have faced—those which I believe will strike a chord with other spouses of persons with MPD. As with so many other illnesses, diseases, and disorders, it is important to know "you are not alone!"

Because an overwhelmingly larger number of women are diagnosed with MPD than men, the spouse I am referring to will typically be the husband. But any feelings and problems experienced in the life of a husband whose wife has MPD would probably also be experienced by a wife whose husband has the disorder, so my observations should be applicable.

I remember the second session with my wife's therapist, a few days after she had been diagnosed with MPD. He said, "There is bad news and good news about MPD. The bad news is, it is the most bizarre and scary form of mental disorder. The good news is, it is one of the most treatable disorders, and she can be completely well within a few years." And he was right! I am grateful to God or fate, or whatever forces brought me to accompany my wife to that first session eight months ago.

That was when I first saw my wife switch to one of her strong alters, and when I first heard her refer to herself in the third person. It certainly qualified as "bizarre," and I might have had a very difficult time believing the diagnosis if I hadn't watched her switch with my own two eyes. Since that first day, bizarre and scary things have happened, and I sometimes have wondered if she really has MPD at all, or if she was just crazy.

It is likely that, just as the person with MPD has to overcome her own distrust of the diagnosis and learn to accept that she really *does* have multiplicity, the spouse must also have a great deal of trust in the therapist, and must overcome any disbelief he might have about her condition. This may be more or less easy, depending on how long she has been in therapy, and how radical her "mood swings" have been in the past.

I have noticed the same sort of denial in spouses that the person with MPD evidences for the first few months: "She couldn't have MPD . . . I have never seen her do anything weird!" "Maybe she is just making this all up to get attention!" "You aren't crazy! You are never going back to that doctor again!"

In my first few dazed days after the initial diagnosis, I forced myself to recall some other things that her doctor had said. *MPD is NOT Schizophrenia. It is NOT insanity. She is NOT crazy.* That was important for me to hear, not only for myself, but for my wife's sake as well. Because during the course of the next few months, she tried to talk *herself* out of her MPD diagnosis, explaining to me that she really *had* made it all up, or that she really had Borderline Personality Disorder, or that she was crazy.

The thoughts that were going through my mind were, "Why, if she has had this condition all her life, is she just *now* having these strange incidents? Why did she wait until *now* to do things like dye her hair blonde and not remember it? Why is she just *now* starting to switch so blatantly between five different alters all within a few minutes? Why is it just *now* that she can sometimes drive without her thick glasses?" There have been times within the past few months that she wanted to stop seeing her psychologist because she said she had just been lying to us all, and didn't really have MPD. It became my responsibility to assure her that she really did have it, and that she needed to continue the therapy even if she didn't think it applied to her.

In the early days after her diagnosis, we had to decide whom to tell. Should we tell her family? My family? Our friends at church? My wife is a very good bridge player, and often competes in tournaments with other partners. Did we need to tell each partner, just in case she switched during a tournament (what if the alter didn't know how to play bridge at all?).

Fortunately we discovered that, although there is almost a total mis-conception on the part of most people about MPD, most of them are genuinely interested, open-minded, and even fascinated to learn the truth about this disorder. Even my wife's mother-in-law (my mother) was very interested in hearing how her therapy was progressing, and was more concerned than shocked. Still, we found it important to be cautious in deciding to whom to divulge this information.

When I met with our minister to tell him what was going on, and why we had to drop out of some time-consuming activities, I was disap-pointed with his reaction to her diagnosis. I told him that she had MPD, and that meant she sometimes did things she didn't remember doing. His response was, "That's pretty convenient." Neither my wife nor I think that her condition is at all convenient for either of us, nor was it convenient for her when she was being abused as a child.

And that, I keep telling her, may be the best reason why I am *sure* she is not "making it all up just to get attention." I can reassure myself, when I have doubts, that nobody would go through the absolute hell of cutting her own arms, of losing friends, of being in the emergency room every month, of being locked into solitary confinement in state mental hospi-tals, in order to "just get attention."

Coming home alone from another hospital admission, to an empty house, an empty bed, an almost deafening silence, may be a welcome respite from the turmoil that is typical of an MPD household. But the spouse is left alone to cope with the fears that his wife is entering unchart-ed territory. He may have seen the look of disbelief on a nurse's face when he admitted her. It said, "Yeah, yeah, you think you have MPD. Well, I'm gonna address you by your *real* name, no matter what you *say* your name is, honey." Unless the treatment facility specializes in MPD, he may hear yet another psychiatrist tell him, "Well, your wife has Atypical Depression with Psychotic Features. We'll keep her here for a while and try some different medications. . . ."

For the spouse of a person with MPD, there are few, if any simple answers. Her doctor doesn't even know how many alters she has. There may be many layers of personalities. I laugh now at how I used to think my wife only had seven or eight. Then it grew to fifteen or twenty. Then we found out they were organized in entire systems.

It isn't very reassuring to know that most psychiatrists were taught in school that MPD is extremely rare. That's like hearing that only six doc-tors in the entire country know how to treat your brain tumor, and you are entering surgery tomorrow to have it removed by someone who thinks he knows how to perform the operation because he read about it in a book! If you are unfortunate enough to have to admit your wife to a hospital on an emergency basis, without any knowledge of its experience in handling MPD, you may be in for a wide range of responses from the hospital staff. We have seen many forms of rejection of her diagnosis. "I'm sorry, but MPD is extremely rare. She's just depressed." "Oh, look, she's decided to have a stomach ache."

Particularly frightening to a spouse is the medical community's presumption that they automatically know more about your wife than you do, when in fact you know good and well that they probably don't even believe in MPD. How often have I heard responses from nurses in an emergency room or state hospital like, "Just wait out here, Mr. M. We'll have a little talk with your wife and observe her for a while . . . ," or "You can go on home and we'll call you."

A spouse who is committed to his wife's recovery can and should be part of her treatment, and should not be excluded from it on the basis that he is not a professional.

In fact, in outpatient treatment situations, the spouse spends twenty-four hours a day with his wife, while the therapist may only see her a few hours a week. Often I have been able to give the therapist information about things which my wife could not recall. Once, while my wife was in the hospital, I received a call in the middle of the night from one of her alters who was terrified and didn't know where she was. She thought she had been committed somewhere, and I had to reassure her that she was in a safe place, and tell her which nurses were "safe" to talk to. (Those that would respect her alters and believe her.)

Another aspect of MPD which has been discussed often on television documentaries and in the literature is that, since most people are finally diagnosed with MPD after having been in treatment for many years, their insurance benefits are usually already exhausted. This occurs just at a time when they need to have very large resources. In my wife's case, it turned out that she had been victimized by a satanic cult every full moon. That explained why, every month, at the same time, she ended up in an emergency room somewhere. A new hospital bill every month! Doctors who treat MPD are faced with a difficult challenge, and should be paid well for their work. They are essentially treating several different people at the same time—people who may be in an almost constant state of crisis that requires the doctor's after-hours and weekend time. A therapist who is seeing a patient with MPD cannot simply refuse to see his patient during a suicidal period just because her insurance benefits have run out.

Just from my own observations, MPD diagnoses will increase exponentially over the next few years as more and more people realize why they have been miserable for so long. Nine months ago I didn't know a single person with MPD. Now I have met twenty or more just in our city. Most of them are in the same predicament: lengthy prior treatment has exhausted their finances, just when they need them most.

It is time for a concerted effort to educate insurance companies that nervous and mental limits should be increased to handle this type of treatment. It is time to ask those who have financial resources in this country to set up foundations to provide scholarships to patients who are unable to pay for the lengthy treatment themselves. Often it is a matter of life or death.

The spouse of a person with MPD is wise to be alert for danger signs as the treatment progresses. Because the treatment involves the recall of traumatic events, and the reversal of amnesia, the patient will get worse before she gets better. There have been several instances when I was watching television and my wife was in the bedroom, and I felt a sudden need to check on her, much as a mother who senses that her children are being "much too quiet." When I check, and discover that she is trying to hang herself in the closet, or is cutting herself, or is standing in the corner dissociated, I realize that vigilance is required.

My first reaction is to get angry that she would attempt to hurt herself. But if I am introspective, I know that I am angry because I am scared that she may succeed in killing herself to alleviate the painful memories, and that I will have lost the best friend I ever had. So, I try to comfort her and support her, rather than showing anger.

Because MPD is typically caused by physical or sexual abuse in childhood, there are often child alters who "need" to be abused in order to feel worthy or loved. It would be interesting to find out how many spouses of people with MPD have been drawn into B&D or Sadomasochistic experiences by their mate, or, indeed, who married that person because they were a willing accomplice to the underlying needs. In our case, once my wife began having flashbacks to her (until then unknown) childhood abuse, we ceased any activities that could be considered abusive, but that seemed to only accelerate her own self-destructiveness. The spouse is then placed in a position of believing that he could remedy her self-damaging behavior by returning to the earlier life-style.

212

While in a "normal" adult relationship, that might be possible, since child alters are involved, it just sets up more difficult situations.

In my wife's case, one of her child alters often appears during love-making, which, for anyone with a sense of morality, presents a severe dilemma. Is this just repeating the child's earlier sexual violations, or can I safely ignore the alter, and continue as if she were the real age of her body? It is particularly difficult in light of the fact that the child alter may make sexual advances or attempt to seduce the spouse, because early in life she was taught by an abusive adult that she would be loved only if she did so. The spouse must understand the consequences of keeping the child alter in this behavioral pattern.

Sometimes the spouse cannot express anger to his mate with MPD because she "short-circuits" the expression of anger by taking it out on herself. Because earlier in life she decided that anything that made an adult angry must have been her own fault, now, in her marriage, if her spouse gets angry, she may withdraw and cut on herself or otherwise hurt herself as "punishment." This sets up a vicious circle where the husband learns that it is not OK to express anger to his wife, and so bottles it up. The pent-up anger manifests itself in inappropriate explosions, which only reinforce the MPD patient's feeling of being at fault. ("It's all my fault. If I weren't always depressed, you would be happier.")

People with MPD may have alters whose sole purpose is to carry out sexual activities. And they do this with single-minded determination. One of my wife's alters named Jeanette has a two word vocabulary, the first of which is a four-letter word, and the second is "me." But the other alters get upset when I ask for Jeanette to come out, because they think I am taking advantage of her. Knowing an alter's name gives one control, and this power should not be abused just for the spouse's own satisfaction.

Presumably when two people get married, they have some idea of what their mate is going to be like for the rest of his or her life. True, each person changes with time, and the spouse must be willing to accept those changes and continue to be committed to his spouse. But, in the case where one of the mates has MPD, the spouse is left with a feeling that he doesn't really know what his wife is going to be like when she "comes out on the other side." What was once a sometimes fearful, sometimes bold, sometimes cautious, sometimes impulsive, sometimes friendly, sometimes cold person, is now a *total* unknown. Will she end up being bold, brash, and impulsive? Will I still like her, or will we no longer be attracted to each other?

In my case, I believe I know the answer. One of these days, the caterpillar that crawled into the cocoon of therapy will emerge a butterfly. What she will look like, I do not know. But I know many of the personalities that make up her system of alters. I have made friends with them, and I feel they trust me. I do not like what some of them have done to her, but I think I understand why they had to do it. I don't hold them responsible for her original pain, and I am glad she had them to rescue her from the torment of her childhood. Now I am waiting for them to all come together, to break out of the cocoon, to put together the puzzle that so many of us, her family and friends, have been anxiously watching.

I know the road is long and hard, and there are times when I can't hold her hand. I have faith in her therapists, psychologists, and psychiatrists, some of whom are groping their way in the dark newness of this disorder. But I know, because I know "all of her," that she will emerge a beautiful butterfly.

Affirmations for Families Coping With MPD

By Robert A.

Believe all of what you hear.
Don't search for proof or details; what's needed will be remembered.
Just take it one day at a time.
No two cases are alike.
Cherish the children . . . but be sure to welcome and respect all alters.
Good or bad, this too shall pass.
I am not their therapist!
Forgive yourself for your fumbles.
　　　. . . and, maybe most important . . .
　　　"DON'T TAKE IT PERSONALLY!"
I also have another suggestion. If you're not familiar with how Twelve Step Fellowships function, simply attend an "Open Meeting" of Alcoholics Anonymous and ask someone there for pointers. Any experienced AA or Al-Anon member will be happy to help you. (Robert A. is the founder of D-D Anon, Group 1, see Resource Guide.)

I'm a part of Diane and I consider myself a significant other. My advice is: be the best friend that you can possibly be. Don't feel that because you don't understand what is happening, that you should just give up the friendship.

Friends don't need to understand everything; they just need to be there to hold a hand or lend a nonjudgmental ear. Most importantly, don't be ashamed to have a friend who has MPD. —Diane H.

I've found it is often helpful to make friends with the presenting alter and rise to the occasion by offering whatever is needed. Talk to and respond to the personality as would be done in any ordinary conversation. Although this can feel jarring and strange (for example, if one suddenly finds oneself face-to-face with a very frightened four-year-old child in an obviously grown-up body), it also offers an opportunity to utilize the exquisitely suggestible and sensitive state of the host to his/her advantage by putting a great deal of love, nurturing, and positive thoughts into their being.

While there may be frustration in the knowledge that this is probably only palliative, it nevertheless can at least minimize the suffering of the moment.

One's gestures *must* be sincere, from the heart, even if one may not feel particularly able to give at the time. Humoring the alter will not suffice, as the alter can sense this. It is sometimes difficult to find the delicate balance between reaching out and being evocative or penetrating, while taking care not to push too far into memories best left alone.

My friend(s) is a wonderful and gifted person. I would love, someday, to see her become whole in oneness. —Iris Y

A Mother Reflects

By Jo C.

I am the mother of a man with MPD. He has successfully completed seven years in treatment, is now happily married, totally integrated, and joyfully looking forward to the life he has wanted for a very long time.

I am grateful that he finally came in contact with some therapists who not only cared about him, but who also understood dissociation and how to help the dissociated patient.

The friends and families of MPD patients are probably very aware of the apparent mood swings—the fact that they are warm and friendly sometimes, but indifferent and possibly abusive other times.

If significant others are supportive and loving family members, they have felt that something was wrong, but weren't sure just what it was.

If the MPD person is an adult, chances are he/she has been in therapy before, with minimal results, and with more severe behavior problems appearing over time.

When friends or family finally learn that the diagnosis is multiple personality disorder, they will probably be either shocked or relieved. Either way, I'll bet the diagnosis made sense!

My son had committed a major crime just prior to the correct diagnosis being made. We had been somewhat estranged and absolutely unable to live together for some time. But when he was arraigned and in so much trouble, I saw him and realized he could not remember how he got in such a mess.

At that point, I knew that I had some very important decisions to make right away. First, did I love him enough to face everything ahead and walk with him through it all, fully supportive of him; whatever happened? Second, could I satisfy my personal bias about mental illness and remain completely open about what had happened?

Because I loved my son very much in spite of our differences and because I felt so strongly about any type of mental illness being dealt with in the open to battle prevailing prejudice, my answer had to be a passionate YES! The criminal justice system was not going to get him if I could help it!

And it didn't. He stayed in the system just long enough to receive treatment from a very astute therapist. He was lucky, too, because he had a wonderful ISH to help as well.

What would I say to the families and friends of a multiple?

1) Keep on loving them! Support their courage over and over again because their path will be very, very painful and lonely at times.

2) Understand when they need to be alone. They are probably dealing with some issues and/or new knowledge and awareness.

3) Learn everything you can about Multiple Personality Disorder. Don't be afraid to ask questions. Your MPD person will let you know if

he/she don't want to discuss something. Just understand that they need to know that the people around them care and understand.

4) If you came from a dysfunctional family and feel that some of your own behavior contributed at least to the prolongation of the disorder: grieve, learn as much as you can, and keep loving your MPD person. Very likely, you have changed from the dysfunctional way you handled your family or disciplined them when they were children. If you are a caring person, you too, will be walking through a lot of your own pain. Don't be afraid, but know that everything that you invest now will be more than worthwhile when you see that person new, shining, and joyous with the new life that they were born to have. You, too, will emerge much changed.

Love is the word. So is *learning* and *understanding*. But *joy* will be the outcome.

A Daughter's Story

By Ann F.

I lived most of my life not knowing that my mother suffered from multiple personality and post traumatic stress as a result of childhood sexual abuse.

I knew she had terrible headaches which caused her to withdraw to her room and speak to no one.

I knew she was quite forgetful at times and often I could not talk to her because she didn't appear to be listening or to know what I had said.

These times were painful and confusing for me. As a child, I felt abandoned and frightened when she was not there for me. She did so many things to make me feel loved and secure that her absences were doubly disturbing.

The headaches and absences became more frequent and noticeable as she grew older. In her late seventies, my mother stopped reading and watching television. She had spells of being very anxious and confused. Doctors called it Alzheimer's or Organic Brain Syndrome.

I knew their diagnoses were wrong. I knew she could still read but didn't want to or was afraid. When I asked her what was wrong, she often answered: "Read about it!"

The media at the time was preoccupied with child abuse, particularly child sexual abuse which was finally coming out of the closet.

After she was hospitalized several times for fractured bones from osteoporosis and had a bout with tubercular meningitis which left her speech impaired, she grew steadily worse. At times she seemed to be hallucinating—both hearing voices and seeing things that I could not see.

She had always been a gentle, composed, courteous person. Now there were extreme moods of fear and anger. She called out words that didn't fit with the situation. She swore, and sometimes attacked those of us who cared for her, pinching and hitting. On one occasion, she threw a tape recorder at our cat who was innocently licking its hind quarters.

I took care of her at home, with help from hired aides, while continuing my career. The financial and emotional drain was tremendous. She became more dependent, requiring a great deal of physical care. A nursing home was an unthinkable alternative. I was determined to understand her and felt a compelling need to protect her from the outside world which labelled her as "senile" or "brain damaged."

I could tell that her intelligence was intact. But she seemed totally helpless, as if she did not know who or where she was. She was different from hour to hour, never showing the same behavior for very long. One moment she was ranting about dirt on the floor and the next, speaking like a little girl, saying: "I love you."

One day a woman from our church stopped in to help me. Barbara was an artist, a poet, a sensitive, creative person who felt a special bond with my mother. She came every week to help and pray with us. One day Barbara said to me: "Do you realize there is more than one person here?" I knew immediately how right she was and wondered why I had not seen it before. Multiple Personality was something I had heard about but had never seen, despite years of work as a therapist in mental health settings. Barbara had been married to a man who had MPD. She began to work with my mother through the medium of art. My mother was eighty-four years old and just beginning her therapy.

During the year that Barbara worked with her, most of the personalities were identified and we began to know and relate to each one. There were three children. Each disclosed a different aspect of the sexual abuse and revealed the perpetrator, a paternal uncle.

My mother, Vera, was locked in her "beautiful room" unaware of any of the abuse. We recognized the anxiety, anger, and "hallucinations."

When Barbara had to leave the state to care for her own ill mother,

I found a therapist who specialized in treating victims of sexual abuse. This skillful, compassionate woman was willing to travel forty-five miles each way, to our home, to treat my mother each week.

Between therapy sessions, I did my best to carry on the work, keeping careful notes, and often calling the therapist for advice.

I was often angry and discouraged, perpetually tired and sometimes terrified, but the steady progress and the wealth of history she gave kept me going.

Not to be underestimated was my excitement and gratification at really knowing my mother and understanding that my terror of abandonment as a child was due to Mother's dissociation.

Our friends and family pretty much backed off during these times. They did not want to believe either the abuse or the Multiple Personality and persisted in thinking she was "brain damaged." (This intelligent, creative woman could remember every detail of her life back to age 3!)

Some came to accept and believe it, but they find it unpleasant to visit us for very long.

My mother is now eighty-seven years old and about to integrate. It is a stormy time for us but it is *happening* and I would not have missed it for anything. I have come to love every one of her eleven personalities, even those who are eminently unlovable and villainous. They all tell the story of her courage and creativity in keeping herself alive and loving despite the cruelty and indifference she suffered as a child. I have only the deepest respect and admiration for my mother.

I salute you Vera, Father, Frank, Mrs. F., Nancy, Ethel, Susan, Boy, Mary, Little Vera, and Baby. Your struggles, which you have allowed me to witness and share to some extent, have given me strength, wisdom, and real comprehension of my roots. The relationships among the members of your "family" are a living drama, spelling out the nature of human beings and the interplay of good and evil, love and hate, in all our lives. One is never too old to find oneself and it is especially important to put our lives in perspective, to know who we are and where we have been before we die.

MPD Is Our Household Word

By Marlene S.

In my opinion, there is nothing simple to say to significant others of people with MPD.

The first and everlasting thing I try to remember is, "this is not about me." I am not part of the problem. I am part of the solution.

My partner's diagnosis is new, so we are sort of flying by the seat of our pants. In our ten years together we have developed the habit of talking things out. I believe this is a real plus for us now, in keeping the current part of the relationship going.

I have found that a deep spiritual connection with my Higher Power is an *absolute necessity*. I must have a way of processing my own issues. I lean on this, because my needs for love, security and understanding don't stop because my partner is emotionally and physically unavailable to me.

I have also found that I have to nurture all the areas of my life (my diet, exercise, and recreation) to be balanced and able to deal with the stress. This is very difficult, but I work toward it because I know its importance.

A satisfying job is a must. At times I have found it is restful to go to work and have a totally different focus. It is not healthy to lose myself in the MPD.

I anticipate that my partner and I will be together for many more years. I love her deeply and she loves me. She is not weird, sick, or a monster. She does not intentionally try to hurt me or sabotage our relationship. She endured every kind of pain since the beginning of her life, and she has survived.

I see her as beautiful, creative, brilliant, and a real asset in my life. I am developing relationships with her alters and giving them the love, attention, and respect they deserve. To say the least, life is never dull!

As a supportive friend or significant other, we can participate in our loved one's recovery by providing a safe, nurturing and stable environment.

Read a lot. Learn all you can. Your partner's therapist can recommend the most current literature. I have found *Multiple Personality Disorder: Diagnosis, Clinical Features, and Treatment* by Colin A. Ross, M.D. to be most helpful.

I believe that family/marital therapy and individual therapy are essential for partners and family members of persons with MPD. Those with MPD will sometimes behave in hurtful, abusive ways. You must learn how to set limits and how to respond to an abusive alter. It helps to remember that the hostile, abusive alter may be just a child who is hurt, angry, or fearful.

Develop a support group and maintain friendships. Your partner cannot always be there for you and may not be able to meet your emotional needs. Take good care of yourself, mentally, physically, and emotionally.

My partner courageously survived a cruel and violent childhood, and relives her pain almost daily. I am challenged and inspired to share this journey with her. Courage and compassion will see us through.
—Phyllis W.

Support for Support People

By Louise's Friend

1. Prior information on MPD is most important.

2. A meeting with the patient's counselor is beneficial, to help with guidelines, expectations, and specifics for "listening time."

3. Significant others must be committed and must learn never to shade the truth. MPD patients are extraordinarily sensitive, and will pick up untruths. (Support people also need to be reassured. I was terrified at first of saying or doing the wrong thing.)

4. We must learn to ask questions in various ways in order to get the patient to respond, and tell us about the counseling. We must overcome our sensitivities to frequent rejection by the patient.

5. We must learn to handle feelings of inadequacy and helplessness when seeing our MPD friend suffering and in pain. When it's someone you love and care about, you want to make the pain go away. Dealing with my anger was hard.

6. I would like it if the counselor (or his secretary) would call at intervals to inform me of difficulties, special needs, or ways to help. I would like to be more aware of special needs.

7. Never once did I question the validity of the abuse. It was only God's grace that enabled me to listen to it. I am thankful for the oppor-

tunity to be a support person. Since Louise's diagnosis, our friendship has grown and a stronger bond has been created.

I think it is important for friends and family to know that MPD is not a sickness or an abnormal way of living, but a creative, brave, and strong way of coping with a lifetime of abuse.

Instead of blaming the person with MPD for something that they did, family and friends should recognize that it was done *to* him/her.

Always be accepting, even if things sound crazy or bizarre. Always be supportive, even if you are scared or confused.

Write everything down—it is amazing how things fit together and begin to make sense.

Be patient. If you think it is hard for you, just think of what the multiple has endured and is enduring.

MPD is just something to work through, like depression, or alcoholism, or any of the other difficult things that go on in this world. It is not a death sentence; you will survive. And, most importantly, so will the person with MPD. Make sure you let them know that—every week, every day, every hour, if necessary. Always keep hope, even in the face of doubt, sadness, fear, and rage.

My significant other is the best thing that has ever happened to me. If it weren't for her ability to survive horrible, unexplainable, inhumane torture and abuse, my life would not be so rich. She is a gift, a wonder— not just to me, but to all the people whose lives she has touched.
—a friend of Lisa's

Sometimes being the partner of a person with MPD can be very lonely. The times that have been the most difficult are when I have spent so much time and energy grieving for our past relationship that I can't see the beauty and strength in our many new relationships.

Many of these relationships have given me the opportunity to be a parent, which I *truly* treasure. I am being given the chance to experience a lot of different things in this world.

Because MPD is a "twenty-four-hour-a-day" thing, those of us who love an MPD are surrounded by it as well. I have found that I cannot be loving and supportive without taking care of myself first. I think it's very important to create space for yourself and to nurture yourself, when living with MPD. —Anonymous

I'm Married to a Person, Not a Label

By John P.

These are my thoughts about my wife, who is called a multiple, and about multiplicity.

I am married to a person, not a label. Placing a label (or making a diagnosis) of MPD on my wife does not change her; it only makes understanding her uniqueness easier.

My wife has amazing capacities as a result of her multiplicity. She seems at home doing almost anything, from hosting a formal dinner, to using ropes during a technical ascent of a vertical rock wall. I envy her ability to fit so well into any situation. Usually in an unfamiliar situation, *I* am the "sore thumb" unless I tag along with her.

Occasionally a flashback may be triggered and a different personality may emerge. Most of the time I am not aware that it has happened. If the personality acts in a way that seems fearful, gentleness usually is the best course for me to take.

My wife was sexually abused, so starting sex can be a problem. Again, gentleness is usually the key.

I have found that if I put *love* and *understanding* into the "system," rather than fear or apprehension, then I am able to tap into the amazing powers that my wife has; these powers can be used to make *me* look like a very perceptive and smart person.

The obvious conclusion is that if I show my wife love, kindness, and compassion, then her multiplicity is a benefit to me, and a plus for our relationship . . . not a liability.

My wife has multiple personalities, but she does *not* have a "disorder." The "disorder" is what *caused* her multiplicity.

Issues of Control

By Thomas R.

I found out that my wife was a multiple on November 10, 1976. At that time, almost nothing was known about this condition. In fact, I had to convince the experts that she was a multiple.

I am sure most therapists know this by now, but it is important for them to realize how stressful MPD is on the patient, the family, and also on the therapist. I also believe that the family of MPDs can cope better if they have more information available to them.

The hardest thing for me to cope with was the sexual indiscretions of the various personalities, along with fear for their safety as they spent many evenings bar-hopping and driving under the influence. A trip across the country and back in a semi-truck was not easy either.

I would like to know the best way to deal with an MPD who does not want help and fights against it. How do you cope with an MPD when integration is viewed as death by the personalities? What do you do when a MPD stops therapy for over three years, keeps the other personalities from coming out, and does not wish to discuss MPD or contribute ideas on the subject?

I would also like to know what family members should not do that could be a hindrance to a multiple, and what things the family can do to help.

Finally, I would like any and all information that would help me understand MPD.

To other friends and supportive family members of individuals with MPD, I would like to say, "You are not alone." Do not hesitate to get counseling for yourself if the stress of coping gets too great.

GLOSSARY

abreaction The discharge of energy involved in recalling an event that has been repressed because it was consciously intolerable. The experience is one of reliving the trauma as if it were happening in the present, complete with physical as well as emotional manifestations. A therapeutic effect sometimes occurs through partial discharge or desensitization of the painful emotions and increased insight.[1] Abreaction can happen spontaneously (see also *flashbacks*), or can be therapeutically induced through verbal suggestion or hypnosis.

acting out Expression of unconscious feelings in actions rather than words. Acting out can take many forms, such as self-inflicted violence or suicidal gestures.

alter Also known as a "personality." Defined as "an entity with a firm, persistent, and well-founded sense of self, and a characteristic and consistent pattern of behavior and feelings in response to given stimuli. It must have a range of functions, a range of emotional responses, and a significant life history (of its own existence)."[2] Many multiples have alters which may be characterized in typical presentations, such as child personalities of various ages, cross-gender personalities, helpers, persecutors, etc. See also *host* and *inner self-helper*.

boundaries For the comfort and safety of the client, therapist, and other outsiders, behavioral boundaries often need to be firmly established. These limits may effect a range of issues: from details of personal and therapeutic interactions, such as length of therapy sessions, appropriate touching, and numbers and duration of phone calls, to prevention of assault or suicide.

contracts Verbal or written agreements made between therapist and client for the express purposes of setting safe and reasonable boundaries for the client, to nurture the client's sense of cause and effect, and to encourage the internal system to take responsibility for its behavior.

dissociation A complex process of changes in a person's consciousness which causes a disturbance or alteration in the normally integrative functions of identity, memory, thoughts, feelings, and experiences. Dissociative processes exist on a continuum. At one end are mild dissociative experiences common to most people (such as day dreaming or highway hypnosis) to the other extreme of severe, chronic dissociation (such as in MPD and other Dissociative Disorders), which may result in an inability to function. Dissociation is normal in children and may be the only effective defense available to them against extreme anxiety caused by highly traumatic situations and acute physical and emotional pain (most commonly sexual abuse). Over time, for a child who has been repeatedly abused, dissociation becomes reinforced and conditioned. See also *Dissociative Disorders*.

Dissociative Disorders A group of psychiatric conditions which share certain common features and which are not due to an Organic Mental Disorder or any other disorder:

> **Psychogenic Amnesia** The sudden inability to recall important personal information too extensive to be explained by ordinary forgetfulness.

> **Psychogenic Fugue** Sudden unexpected travel away from one's home or place of work, with the assumption of a new identity and the inability to remember one's past.

> **Depersonalization Disorder** Persistent or recurrent episodes of depersonalization (in which the usual sense of one's own reality is lost or changed) sufficiently severe to caused marked distress.

> **Multiple Personality Disorder** The existence of two or more distinct personalities, each of which is dominant at a given time. The dominant personality determines the individual's behavior. Each personality has a consistent pattern of perceiving the environment and self.

> **Dissociative Disorder Not Otherwise Specified** A category of disorders which predominantly features dissociative symptoms, but which does not meet the criteria for the specific Dissociative Disorders previously listed.[3]

flashbacks A type of spontaneous abreaction common to victims of acute trauma. Also known as "intrusive recall," flashbacks have been categorized into four types:

1) dreams or nightmares, 2) dreams from which the dreamer awakens but remains under the influence of the dream content and has difficulty making contact with reality, 3) conscious flashbacks, in which the person may or may not lose contact with reality and which may be accompanied by multimodal hallucinations, and 4) unconscious flashbacks, in which the person "relives" a traumatic event with no awareness at the time or later of the connection between the flashback and the past trauma.[4]

fugue See *Dissociative Disorder, Psychogenic Fugue*.

fusion The process of breaking down the dissociative barriers that segregate individual alter personalities. One may experience a "partial fusion," or consolidation of clusters of alters into a few discrete personalities. The fusion process lays the groundwork for integration.[5] See also *integration*.

host The alter that most frequently has "control" of the body. The host is often initially unaware of the other alters and typically *loses time* when they appear. He/she is the alter that most often initiates treatment, generally after experiencing a range of psychological and somatic symptoms, most frequently depression.

hypnosis A person's ability to respond to appropriate suggestions by altering perception or memory. Dissociation itself is a form of self-hypnosis. Hypnosis is one of the most important adjunctive methods of MPD treatment, most commonly used to facilitate contact with alters, to overcome amnesic blocks, and to promote healing through managed abreaction.

inner self-helper (ISH) An alter among the typical group of helper or protector personalities. Therapists have found ISHs present in the majority of individuals diagnosed with MPD. Generally, an ISH has complete information and a good understanding of the workings of the system.

integration A complete unification or "stable" *fusion* which the person can maintain on a long-term or permanent basis. Some clinicians consider integration crucial to the resolution of treatment, others don't. The therapist and client together should weigh the relative merits of a cooperative group versus a single entity, and set their goals accordingly.

losing time Having no recollection of what one did during a given time period (hours, days, even years). Unaccounted for periods may be the most frightening and dangerous aspect of the dissociative defense in adults. Time loss allows the potential for re-victimization of an individual who has MPD.

switching The process of changing from one alter personality to another. Switching may be stimulated by an internal perception of the need for a particular alter or by an external, environmental *trigger*. Individuals with MPD have varying degrees of control over the process, gaining more control as treatment progresses.

Switches may be accompanied by physiological changes (such as posture, facial expressions, and voice or speech patterns) and by psychological changes (such as mood, behavioral age, and level of intelligence).[6]

system The structure of relationships within the internal world of an individual who has MPD. Although each person's system is unique, there are several recurring metaphors that MPD clients use to describe how they function. Examples include stages, spotlights, tunnels, houses, and levels. It is often helpful for a person with MPD to make a map or diagram of his/her internal personality system.

transference "The unconscious assignments to others of feelings and attitudes that were originally associated with important figures in one's early life." The psychodynamically oriented clinician uses this to help the client understand the origins of emotional problems.[7] The transference phenomena is complicated in MPD because each alter may have its own transference relationship with the therapist.

trauma A medical term for any sudden injury or damage to an organism. Psychological trauma is an event that is outside the range of usual human experience and which is so seriously distressing as to overwhelm the mind's defenses and cause lasting emotional harm.

Psychological traumata include natural disasters, accidents, or human actions which cause the victim to be terrified, helpless, and under extreme physical stress.[8] Most individuals with MPD have been victims of repeated child abuse, rape, and/or torture, but other kinds of psychological trauma, including severe neglect, can also cause MPD.

trigger An event, object, person, etc. that sets a series of thoughts in motion or reminds a person of some aspect of their traumatic past. The person may be unaware of what is "triggering" the memory (ie., loud noises, a particular color, piece of music, odor, etc.). Connected with brainwashing, a trigger may elicit a specific command message.

[1]Stone, Evelyn M., ed., *American Psychiatric Glossary*, Washington, D.C.: American Psychiatric Press, 1988, 1.

[2]Kluft, Richard. An Introduction to Multiple Personality Disorder, *Psychiatric Annals*, (1984) 14: 19-24.

[3]*Diagnostic and Statistical Manual of Mental Disorders, (Third Edition, Revised)*, Washington, D.C.: American Psychiatric Press, 1987, 269-277.

[4]Putnam, Frank W., *Diagnosis and Treatment of Multiple Personality Disorder*, NY: Guilford Press, 1989, 236-237.

[5] Putnam, 301-302.

[6] Putnam, p. 117-122.

[7] Stone, p. 168.

[8] DSM-III-R, p. 247-248.

RESOURCES

The resources listed here are not necessarily endorsed by the editors of this volume, but are intended to give people a starting place for their own exploration into the programs, organizations, and publications available to MPD and Dissociative Disorders survivors, their therapists, and supportive family members.

MPD and DD Treatment Programs

Listed alphabetically by state

Center for Dissociative Disorders
College Hospital
10802 College Place
Cerritos, CA 90701

National Center for the Treatment of Dissociative Disorders
4495 Hale Parkway, Suite 180
Denver, CO 80220

HCA Columbine Psychiatric Center
8565 South Poplar Way
Littleton, CO 80126

229

Charter Peachford Hospital (program especially for child and adolescent MPD)
2151 Peachford Road
Atlanta, GA 30338
800/451-2151

The Center For Dissociative Disorders
Ridgeview Institute
3995 South Cobb Drive
Smyrna, GA 30080-6397
800/345-9775

Dissociative Disorders Program
Rush North Shore Medical Center
9600 Gross Point Road
Skokie, IL 60076

River Oaks Psychiatric Hospital
1525 River Oaks Road West
New Orleans, LA 70123

The Chesapeake Institute
11141 Georgia Avenue, Suite 310
Silver Spring, MD 20902

Sheppard and Enoch Pratt Hospital
6501 North Charles Street
Baltimore, MD 21285

Cottonwood de Albuquerque
804 Blythe Road
Las Lunas, NM 87031
800/877-4519

Trauma and Recovery Program
Akron General Medical Center
400 Wabash Avenue
Akron, OH 44307

Northwestern Institute
450 Bethlehem Pike
Fort Washington, PA 19034

Institute of Pennsylvania Hospital
Dissociative Disorders Unit
111 N. 49th Street
Philadelphia, PA 19139

Quakertown Community Hospital
Eleventh Street and Park Avenue
Quakertown, PA 18951

Charter Hospital of Dallas
Dissociative Disorder Unit
6800 Preston Rd.
Plano, TX 75024

HCA Richland Hospital
7501 Glenview Drive
North Richland Hills, TX 76180

Abuse and Dissociative Disorders Recovery Unit
HCA Dominion Hospital
2960 Sleepy Hollow Road
Falls Church, VA 22044

Non-Profit Organizations, National and International

Healing Hearts
1515 Webster Street
Oakland, CA 94612
Information and referral for survivors of ritual abuse; publishes resource directory of helping professionals; conducts annual survivor conferences.

Incest Survivors Anonymous (ISA)
P.O. Box 5613
Long Beach, CA 90805-0613
213/428-5599
Founded 1980. Self-help peer program for men, women and teens, based on the 12 steps and 12 traditions of Alcoholics Anonymous, adapted to incest.

Incest Survivor Information Exchange (ISIE)
P.O. Box 3399
New Haven, CT 06515
203/389-5166

Incest Survivors Resource Network International (ISRNI)
P.O. Box 7375
Las Cruces, NM 88006-7375
516/935-3031
A Quaker-affiliated, international educational resource devoted to primary prevention of incest.

International Society for the Study of Multiple Personality and Dissociation (ISSMP&D)
5700 Old Orchard Road, First Floor
Skokie, IL 60077-1024
708/966-4322
This is the primary professional organization for therapists who work with MPD and DD. There is an affiliate membership category for interested lay people. The ISSMP&D newsletter includes a bibliography of recent articles and books on MPD and DD. Therapists may wish to inquire about local or regional Component Society Study Groups in their area. Annual conference is primarily for therapists, but may be of interest to clients and their support people.

Looking Up
P.O. Box K
Augusta, ME 04332-0470
207/626-3402
Founded 1984. Serves the needs of non-offending male and female victims and survivors of incest. Services include an Outdoor Challenge Program, annual retreats for survivors, resource referral to providers nationwide, financial assistance for people in crisis, and two publications.

MPD Dignity
P.O. Box 4367
Boulder, CO 80306-4367
A self-help organization exclusively for survivors with Multiple Personality Disorder.

The Onionskin Collective
2315-B Forest Drive, Suite 50
Annapolis, MD 21401
301/263-1151
Supporting the recovery of adult victims of incest and child sexual abuse. Provides: information to survivors, professionals, public and media; consultants to health care providers; support groups; publications; professional training for health care providers; survivor advocacy programs.

P.L.E.A. (Prevention-Leadership-Education-Assistance)
356 West Zia Road
Santa Fe, NM 87505-5723
505/982-9184
Purpose is to combat physical, sexual and emotional abuse of males. Provides nationwide referrals to professionals experienced in helping male survivors. Newsletter, bibliography and speakers' bureau.

Ritual Abuse Information Network
8144 Walnut Hill Lane, Suite 998
Dallas, TX 75231

The Safer Society Program
RR1, Box 24-B
Orwell, VT 05760-9756
802/897-7541
A nationwide project of the New York State Council of Churches. A research, advocacy and referral center which serves as a clearinghouse for newly emerging topics and publisher of research studies and books on the prevention of sexual abuse.

The Sidran Foundation
211 Southway
Baltimore, MD 21218
A public-interest organization devoted to advocacy, education and research on behalf of persons with trauma-induced psychiatric problems, and those undiagnosed, misdiagnosed, and mismedicated patients within the mental health system. Operates The Sidran Press, publisher of this book.

The Survivors of Childhood Abuse Program (SCAP)—a division of
Childhelp USA
6463 Independence Ave.
Woodland Hills, CA 91367
818/347-7280

Objectives include: research, treatment, training, consultation and public education, network of resources and advocacy on behalf of survivors. In addition to survivors of sexual abuse, SCAP serves those who experienced parental substance abuse, domestic violence, neglect, physical and emotional abuse. Publications include a guidebook for survivors.

Survivors of Incest Anonymous, Inc.
World Service Office
P.O. Box 21817
Baltimore, MD 21222-6817
301/282-3400
A self-help group of adult men and women, based on the 12 step Alcoholics Anonymous model. International groups, bimonthly bulletins, pen pals, hotline.

VOICES In Action, Inc. (Victims of Incest Can Emerge Survivors)
P.O. Box 148309
Chicago, IL 606 14
312/327-1500
Survivors and pro-survivors dedicated to prevention and recovery through networking, support and education. Services include: comprehensive bibliography, formats for starting self-help groups, information on selecting a therapist, special interest groups for specific populations of survivors (ie., males, ritual abuse, MPD, etc.), VOICES newsletter, annual conference for survivors, family members and professionals.

ORGANIZATIONS ESPECIALLY FOR SPOUSES AND LOVED ONES OF INDIVIDUALS WITH DISSOCIATIVE DISORDERS

DD-Anon Group One
P.O. Box 4078
Appleton, WI 54911
A mutual-help support group for people who have a spouse, relative or friend in treatment for a dissociative disorder (usually MPD). Program is based on the 12 Step/12 Traditions model of Alcoholics Anonymous. Group is pleased to provide information and support to people wishing to start DD-Anon chapters in other areas.

Loved Ones of Multiples (LOOM)
c/o MPD Dignity
P.O. Box 4367
Boulder, CO 80306-4367

Periodicals

DISSOCIATION: Progress in the Dissociative Disorders
The Journal of the ISSMP&D
c/o Ridgeview Institute
3995 South Cobb Dr.
Smyrna, GA 30080-6397
800/345-9775

THE CUTTING EDGE
A newsletter for people who live with self-inflicted violence
2469 Noble Road #26
Cleveland Heights, OH 44121-2125

FOR CRYING OUT LOUD
A quarterly newsletter by and for women with a sexual abuse history
Cambridge Women's Center
46 Pleasant Street
Cambridge, MA 02139

MANY VOICES
A national bi-monthly self-help publication for persons with Multiple Personalities or Dissociative Disorders
P.O. Box 2639
Cincinnati, OH 45201-2639

MPD REACHING OUT
A newsletter about Multiple Personality Disorder
c/o Public Relations Department
Royal Ottawa Hospital
1145 Carling Avenue
Ottawa, Ontario
Canada K1Z 7K4

SURVIVOR Me2
A bi-monthly creative journal by men and women survivors of sexual assault.
3636 Taliluna, Suite 125
Knoxville, TN 37919
615/637-0869

SURVIVORSHIP
A forum for survivors of ritual abuse and other torture
3181 Mission Street, #139
San Francisco, CA 94110

TRAUMA AND RECOVERY NEWSLETTER
A semi-annual publication promoting the study and treatment of trauma related conditions
c/o Akron General Medical Center
Department of Psychiatry and Behavioral Sciences
400 Wabash Ave.
Akron, OH 44307
216/384-6525

General Information, Audio, and Video Tapes

Audio Archives of Canada
100 West Beaver Creek, Unit 18
Richmond Hill, Ontario L4B 1H4
416/889-6555
Distributes audio tapes of conferences conducted by Education/Dissociation. Contact Education/Dissociation, below, for conference and session information.

Audio Transcripts, Ltd.
335 South Patrick Street
Alexandria, VA 22314
800/338-2111
This company makes audiotapes of the major professional meetings dealing with MPD and dissociation. Their catalog of available tapes is free.

Education/Dissociation
c/o The Muskoka Meeting Place for Counseling and Education
955 Muskoka Road South
Gravenhurst, Ontario P0C 1G0
705/687-7686 or 416/274-9146
Conducts educational conferences and workshops for professionals and the public. Publishes and distributes *Multiple Personality Disorder: Putting Many Faces on Child Abuse* (a video training documentary) and Rivera, *Multiple Personality Disorder: An Outcome of Child Abuse,* Toronto: Education/Dissociation, 1991. (This twenty page booklet, which supports the video, is also sold separately. It is a thorough and concise explaination of MPD written in language accessible to lay readers.)

The Center for Dissociative Disorders
Ridgeview Institute
3995 South Cobb Drive
Smyrna, GA 30080
800/345-9775
Multiple Personality Disorder: An Overview, a 60-minute videotape for medical and professional education (available for purchase or 7-day rental).

Akron General Medical Center
Department of Psychiatry
Attn: Barbara Lohmier
400 Wabash Avenue
Akron, OH 44307
216/384-6525
Multiple Personality and Dissociative States, an extensive bibliography edited by Dr. Moshe S. Torem

Books

The ISSMP&D, listed previously, compiles an on-going and very thorough bibliography of books and articles on the subject of MPD and dissociative disorders. While we cannot attempt to reproduce that lengthy and, in some cases, very specialized list, here are a few key books that will be helpful to clients, spouses, and therapists.

American Psychiatric Association, *Diagnostic and Statistical Manual of Mental Disorders (Third Edition-Revised)*, Washington, D.C., American Psychiatric Press, 1987.

Bass, Ellen and Davis, Laura. *The Courage to Heal: A Guide for Women Survivors of Child Sexual Abuse*. New York, Harper and Row, 1988.

Braun, Bennett G., ed. *Treatment of Multiple Personality Disorder*. Washington, D.C., American Psychiatric Press, 1986.

Courtois, Christine A. *Healing the Incest Wound*. New York, Norton, 1988.

Davis, Laura. *The Courage to Heal Workbook: For Women and Men Survivors of Child Sexual Abuse*. New York, Harper and Row, 1990.

Gil, Eliana. *Outgrowing the Pain: A Book for and about Adults Abused as Children*. CA, Launch Press, 1983.

—*United We Stand: A Book for People with Multiple Personalities*. CA, Launch Press, 1990.

Kluft, Richard. *Childhood Antecedents of Multiple Personality Disorder*. Washington, D.C., American Psychiatric Press, 1985.

—*Incest-Related Syndromes of Adult Psychopathology*. Washington, D.C., American Psychiatric Press, 1990.

Lew, Michael. *Victims No Longer: Men Recovering from Incest and Other Sexual Child Abuse*. New York, Harper and Row, 1988.

Putnam, Frank W. *Diagnosis and Treatment of Multiple Personality Disorder*. New York, Guilford Press, 1989.

Ross, Colin A. *Multiple Personality Disorder: Diagnosis, Clinical Features, and Treatment*. New York, John Wiley and Sons, 1989.

CONTRIBUTORS

A friend of Lisa's 222
"All of Me" & the A-Team 21
Billie A. 59
Charlie A. 100
Kathy A. 12, 30, 52, 92, 106, 160, 196
Robert A. 214
Sharon A. 93, 103, 194
Susan A. 128-131
Aleda 85, 95
Charlie Anderson 155-156, 192
Anonymous 53
Anonymous 151
Anonymous 222
Cindy B. 124, 170, 197
Gregory B. 9-10, 50-51, 56-57, 64-65, 173-175
Kim B. 36, 126, 159, 184
Linda B. 34, 107
Linda B. (& Friends) 198
Lori B. 3, 103, 193-194
Marita B. 163-164
Robin B. (art) 16

Susan B. 125, 158-159, 177
Tina B. 120-121
Tony B. 1, 41, 178-179, 197
Anne C. 40, 92-93, 151
Jan C. 47-48, 168
Jo C. 215-217
Kathy C. 77, 125, 179, 192-193
Lucia C. 144-146
Marsha C. 33, 100, 191
R.C. 34, 132, 170, 182
Susan C. 1, 25, 126, 183-184
Virginia C. 121, 189
Diana D. 18, 201
Jana D. 71-72
Judith D. 28-30
Lynn D. 114-115
Suzanne D. 93-94, 182
Brenda E. 26-27
A.M.F. 205
AMF 109
Ann F. 217-219
Cathy F. 108, 201-203
Janet F. 121-122

240

INDEX

243

245